Workshop on Dialogue in Motion

(DM 2014)

Held at the 14th Conference of the European Chapter of the Association for Computational Linguistics

Gothenburg, Sweden
26 April 2014

ISBN: 978-1-63266-397-9

Printed from e-media with permission by:

Curran Associates, Inc.
57 Morehouse Lane
Red Hook, NY 12571

Printed by Curran Associates, Inc. (2014)

For permission requests, please contact the Association for Computational Linguistics at the address below.

Association for Computational Linguistics
209 N. Eighth Street
Stroudsburg, Pennsylvania 18360

Phone: 1-570-476-8006
Fax: 1-570-476-0860

acl@aclweb.org

Additional copies of this publication are available from:

Curran Associates, Inc.
57 Morehouse Lane
Red Hook, NY 12571 USA
Phone: 845-758-0400
Fax: 845-758-2634
Email: curran@proceedings.com
Web: www.proceedings.com

IBM

Deutsches
Forschungszentrum
für Künstliche
Intelligenz GmbH

SEVENTH FRAMEWORK
PROGRAMME

THE UNIVERSITY OF EDINBURGH

KTH
VETENSKAP
OCH KONST

UNIVERSITY OF
CAMBRIDGE

HERIOT
WATT
UNIVERSITY

NUANCE

YAHOO!
LABS

Introduction

Spoken dialogue systems used in call centers and car dashboards reflect years of technological development. But the smart devices that now accompany people throughout their daily activities and the extensive integration of sensors and actuators into people's environments demand new concepts in dialogue modeling and management in order to provide intuitive, proactive, personalized, context-aware, multi-modal, multi-domain dialogue systems.

The past few years have seen the development of many intelligent speech-enabled virtual assistants for mobile users, such as Siri, S Voice, Google Now, SpeakToIt, Vlingo and Iris. These applications use GIS connectivity for navigation and to contextualize tasks such as search. Other multimodal applications (e.g. Wikitude, WikiHood, FieldTrip) can pro-actively present encyclopedic information about the user's surroundings, such as landmarks and points of interest, as the user walks around. Augmented reality and wearable technology such as Google Glass are presenting new opportunities for dialogue systems 'on the go'.

In this proliferation of location-aware systems in the industry, together with research efforts in spatial and mobile contexts, we see a convergence of efforts (e.g. the Word2Actions workshop at NAACL 2012, the Computational Models of Spatial Language Interpretation and Generation workshop series and the Vision and Language workshop at NAACL 2013) towards what we call **Dialogue In Motion**: any form of interaction between a computer/robot and a human in motion - for example a pedestrian or a driver, in the real world or in a simulated environment. Natural language interactions are promoted as a more direct interaction medium, but they raise additional challenges in the context of dynamic spatial environments. This workshop focuses on these challenging issues in language processing for dialogues in motion.

We received 20 submissions; all papers received three reviews from our program committee. We accepted seven papers for oral presentation and six for poster and/or demo presentation. Several of the papers are on in-car dialogue systems, which have a long track record of non-trivial implementations combining voice, GUI, haptic, and gestures with additional constraints on user's cognitive load and environment context. Others are on pedestrian navigation and virtual guides, human-robot interaction, and rapid prototyping and statistical dialogue management for dialogue in motion.

We wish to thank all those who submitted papers. We also gratefully acknowledge the work of the members of our program committee. Special thanks go to Tiphaine Dalmas (University of Edinburgh) for acting as main contact for the workshop, and to Bonnie Webber (University of Edinburgh) for helpful comments along the way.

We hope you enjoy the workshop!

Dialog in Motion Organising Committee

Tiphaine Dalmas, ILCC, University of Edinburgh (United Kingdom)
Jana Götze, KTH, Royal Institute of Technology (Sweden)
Joakim Gustafson, KTH, Royal Institute of Technology (Sweden)
Srinivasan Janarthanam, Heriot-Watt University (United Kingdom)
Jan Kleindienst, IBM Czech Republic, Prague (Czech Republic)
Christian Mueller, DFKI, Saarbruecken (Germany)
Amanda Stent, Yahoo! Labs, New York (USA)
Andreas Vlachos, University of Cambridge (United Kingdom)

Dialog in Motion Program Committee

Yoav Artzi, University of Washington (USA)
Luciana Benotti, University of Cordoba (Spain)
Johan Boye, KTH Royal Institute of Technology (Sweden)
Stephen Clark, University of Cambridge (United Kingdom)
Jan Curin, IBM Czech Republic, Prague (Czech Republic)
Nina Dethlefs, Heriot-Watt University (United Kingdom)
Jens Edlund, KTH, Stockholm (Sweden)
Dan Goldwasser, University of Maryland (USA)
Joakim Gustafson, KTH, Stockholm (Sweden)
Peter Heeman, OGI, Oregon Health and Science University (USA)
Filip Jurcicek, Charles University, Prague (Czech Republic)
John Kelleher, Dublin Institute of Technology (Ireland)
Kazunori Komatani, Nagoya University (Japan)
Tom Kwiatkowski, University of Washington (USA)
Staffan Larsson, Gothenburg University (Sweden)
Oliver Lemon, Heriot-Watt University (United Kingdom)
Nils Lenke, Nuance Communications, Aachen (Germany)
Jan Macek, IBM Czech Republic, Prague (Czech Republic)
Tomas Macek, IBM Czech Republic, Prague (Czech Republic)
Ray Mooney, University of Texas, Austin (USA)
Deepak Ramachandran, Nuance Communications (USA)
Verena Rieser, Heriot-Watt University (United Kingdom)
Hui Shi, Singapore-MIT Alliance for Research and Technology (Singapore)
Thora Tenbrink, Bangor University (United Kingdom)
Jason Williams, Microsoft Research (USA)

Table of Contents

Conference Program

(09:00-10:30) Session I

09:00-10:00 Invited speaker (TBA)

10:00–10:30 *In-Car Multi-Domain Spoken Dialogs: A Wizard of Oz Study*
Sven Reichel, Ute Ehrlich, André Berton and Michael Weber

(10:30-11:00) Coffee break

(11:00-12:00) Session II

11:00–11:30 *IBM's Belief Tracker: Results On Dialog State Tracking Challenge Datasets*
Rudolf Kadlec, Jindrich Libovicky, Jan Macek and Jan Kleindienst

11:30–12:00 *Click or Type: An Analysis of Wizard's Interaction for Future Wizard Interface Design*
Srinivasan Janarthanam, Robin Hill, Anna Dickinson and Morgan Fredriksson

(13:30-14:30) Posters and demonstrations

Recipes for building voice search UIs for automotive
Martin Labsky, Ladislav Kunc, Tomas Macek, Jan Kleindienst and Jan Vystrcil

A Natural Language Instructor for pedestrian navigation based in generation by selection
Santiago Avalos and Luciana Benotti

Mining human interactions to construct a virtual guide for a virtual fair
Andrés Luna and Luciana Benotti

Collaborative Exploration in Human-Robot Teams: What's in their Corpora of Dialog, Video, & LIDAR Messages?
Clare Voss, Taylor Cassidy and Douglas Summer-Stay

Multi-threaded Interaction Management for Dynamic Spatial Applications
Srinivasan Janarthanam and Oliver Lemon

Mostly Passive Information Delivery – a Prototype
Jan Vystrcil, Tomas Macek, David Luksch, Martin Labsky, Kunc Ladislav, Jan Kleindienst and Tereza Kasparova

No Day Set (continued)

Session 14:30-15:30: Session III

14:30–15:00 *Navigation Dialog of Blind People: Recovery from Getting Lost*
Jan Vystrcil, Ivo Maly, Jan Balata and Zdenek Mikovec

15:00–15:30 *Conversational Strategies for Robustly Managing Dialog in Public Spaces*
Aasish Pappu, Ming Sun, Seshadri Sridharan and Alexander Rudnicky

(15:30-16:00) Coffee break

(16:00-17:00) Session IV

16:00–16:30 *Situationally Aware In-Car Information Presentation Using Incremental Speech Generation: Safer, and More Effective*
Spyros Kousidis, Casey Kennington, Timo Baumann, Hendrik Buschmeier, Stefan Kopp and David Schlangen

16:30–17:00 *Human pause and resume behaviours for unobtrusive humanlike in-car spoken dialogue systems*
Jens Edlund, Fredrik Edelstam and Joakim Gustafson

In-Car Multi-Domain Spoken Dialogs: A Wizard of Oz Study

Sven Reichel, Ute Ehrlich, André Berton
Speech Dialogue Systems
Daimler AG
Ulm, Germany
{sven.reichel, ute.ehrlich, andre.berton}@daimler.com

Michael Weber
Institute of Media Informatics
Ulm University
Germany
michael.weber@uni-ulm.de

Abstract

Mobile Internet access via smartphones puts demands on in-car infotainment systems, as more and more drivers like to access the Internet while driving. Spoken dialog systems support the user by less distracting interaction than visual/haptic-based dialog systems. To develop an intuitive and usable spoken dialog system, an extensive analysis of the interaction concept is necessary. We conducted a Wizard of Oz study to investigate how users will carry out tasks which involve multiple applications in a speech-only, user-initiative infotainment system while driving. Results show that users are not aware of different applications and use anaphoric expressions in task switches. Speaking styles vary and depend on type of task and dialog state. Users interact efficiently and provide multiple semantic concepts in one utterance. This sets high demands for future spoken dialog systems.

1 Introduction

The acceptance of smartphones is a success story. These devices allow people to access the Internet nearly anywhere at anytime. While driving, using a smartphone is prohibited in many countries as it distracts the driver. Regardless of this prohibition, people use their smartphone and cause severe injuries (National Highway Traffic Safety Administration (NHTSA), 2013). In order to reduce driver distraction, it is necessary to integrate the smartphone's functionality safely into in-car infotainment systems. Since hands and eyes are involved in driving, a natural and intuitive speech-based interface increases road safety (Maciej and Vollrath, 2009). There are already infotainment systems with Internet applications like e.g. weather, music streaming, gas prices, news, and restaurant search. However, not all of them can be controlled by natural speech.

In systems based on graphic and haptic modality, the functionality is often grouped into various applications. Among other things, this is due to the limited screen size. The user has to start an application and select the desired functionality. A natural speech interface does not require a fragmentation of functionalities into applications, as people can express complex commands by speech. In single-application tasks, such as calling someone, natural speech interfaces are established and proven. However, users often encounter complex tasks, which involve more than one application. For example, while hearing the news about a new music album, the driver might like to start listening to this album via Internet radio. Spoken language allows humans to express a request such as "Play this album" easily, since the meaning is clear. However, will drivers also use this kind of interaction while using an in-car **s**poken **d**ialog **s**ystem (SDS)? Or is the mental model of application interaction schema dominant in human-computer interaction? In a user experiment, we confront drivers with multi-domain tasks, to observe how they interact.

While interacting with an SDS, one crucial problem for users is to know which utterances the system is able to understand. People use different approaches to solve this problem, for example by reading the manual, using on-screen help, or relying on their experiences. In multi-domain dialog systems, utterances can be quite complex, thus remembering all utterances from the manual or displaying them on screen would not be possible. As a result, users have to rely on their experience in communications to know what to say. Thus, an advanced SDS needs to understand what a user would naturally say in this situation to execute a certain task.

In this paper, we present results from a **W**izard **of** **O**z (WoZ) experiment on multi-domain interaction with an in-car SDS. The goal of this study is to build a corpus and analyze it according to application awareness, speaking styles, anaphoric references, and efficiency. Our results provide a detailed insight how drivers start multi-application tasks and switch between applications by speech. This will answer the question whether they are primed to application-based-interaction or use a natural approach known from human-human-communication. The results will be used to design grammars or language models for working prototypes, which establish a basis for real user tests. Furthermore, we provide guidelines for multi-domain SDSs.

The remainder of this paper is structured as follows: Section 2 provides an overview of other studies in this context. Section 3 describes the domain for the user experiment which is presented in Section 4. Data analysis methods are defined in Section 5. We present the results in Section 6 and discuss them in Section 7. Finally, we conclude and give guidelines for multi-domain SDSs in Section 8.

2 Related Work

Many studies exist which evaluate SDSs concerning performance, usability, and driver distraction (a good overview provides Ei-Wen Lo and Green (2013)). Usually, participants are asked to complete a task, while driving in a simulated environment or in real traffic. Geutner et al. (2002), for example, showed that a virtual co-driver contributes to ease of use with little distraction effects. In their WoZ experiment, natural language was preferred to command-and-control input. However, no in-depth analysis of user utterances is presented. Cheng et al. (2004) performed an analysis of natural user utterances. They observed that drivers, occupied in a driving task, use disfluent and distracted speech and react differently than by concentrating on the speech interaction task. None of the studies provide in-depth analysis of multi-domain tasks, as our work does.

Multi-domain SDS exist like e.g. SmartKom (Reithinger et al., 2003) or CHAT (Weng et al., 2007). They presented complex systems with many functionalities, however, they do not evaluate subtask switching from users' point of view. In CHAT, the implicit application switch was even disabled due to "extra burden on the system". Domain switches are analyzed in human-human communication as e.g. in Villing et al. (2008). However, people interact differently with a system than with a human. Even in human-computer communication, speaking styles differ depending on type of task, as (Hofmann et al., 2012) showed in a web-based user study. In order to develop an intuitive multi-application SDS, it is necessary to analyze how users interact in a driving situation by completing tasks across different domains.

3 User Tasks

In a user experiment it is crucial to set real tasks for users, since artificial tasks will be hard to remember and can reduce their attention. We analyzed current in-car infotainment systems with Internet access and derived eight multi-domain tasks from their functionality (see Table 1). The subtasks were classified according to Kellar et al. (2006)'s web information classification schema in information seeking (Inf), information exchange, and information maintenance. Since information maintenance is not a strong automotive use case, these tasks were grouped together with information exchange. We call them action subtasks (Act) as they initiate an action of the infotainment system (e.g. "turn on the radio").

No	App 1	App 2	App3
1	POI Search	Restaurant	Call
2	Knowledge	Ski Weather	Navigation
3	Weather	Hotel Search	Address book
4	Play Artist	News Search	Forward by eMail
5	Navigation	Restaurant	Save as Favorite
6	News Search	Play Artist	Share on Facebook
7	News Search	Knowledge	Convert Currency
8	Navigation	Gas Prices	Status Gas Tank

Table 1: Multi-application user tasks.

Since only few use cases involve more than three applications, every user task is a story of three subtasks. In task number 5 for example, a user has to start a subtask, which navigates him to Berlin. Then he would like to search an Italian restaurant at the destination. Finally, he adds the selected restaurant to his favorites. The focus is on task entry and on subtask switch, thus the subtasks require only two to four semantic concepts (like *Berlin* or *Italian restaurant*). One of these concepts is a reference to the previous subtask (like *at the destination* or *the selected restaurant*) to ensure a natural cross-application dialog flow. After the system's response for one subtask the user has to initiate the next subtask to complete his task.

4 User Experiment

Developing an SDS means specifying a grammar or training statistical language models for speech recognition. These steps precede any real user test. In system-initiated dialogs, with a few possible utterances, specifying a grammar is feasible. However, in strictly user-initiative dialogs with multiple applications, this is rather complicated. A WoZ study does not require to develop speech recognition and understanding as this is performed by a human. Analyzing the user utterances of a WoZ experiment provides a detailed view of how a user will interact with the SDS. This helps in designing spoken dialogs and specifying grammars and/or training language models for further evaluations (Fraser and Gilbert, 1991; Glass et al., 2000).

Interaction schemes of people vary among each other and depend on age, personality, experience, context, and many more. It is essential to conduct a user study with people who might use the SDS later on. A study by the NHTSA (National Highway Traffic Safety Administration (NHTSA), 2013) showed that in 2011 73% of the drivers involved in fatal crashes due to cell phone use, were less than 40 years old. For this reason, our study considers drivers between 18 and 40 years who are technically affine and are likely to buy a car equipped with an infotainment system with Internet access.

4.1 Experimental Set-Up

When designing a user interaction experiment, it is important that it takes place in a real environment. As driving on a real road is dangerous, we used a fixed-base driving simulator in a laboratory. In front of the car, a screen covers the driver's field of view (see Figure 1). Steering and pedal signals are picked from the car's CAN bus. It is important that the user assumes he is interacting with a computer as "human-human interactions are not the same as human-computer interactions" (Fraser and Gilbert, 1991). The wizard, a person in charge of the experiment, was located behind the car and mouse clicks or any other interaction of the wizard was not audible in the car. To ensure a consistent behavior of the wizard, we used SUEDE (Klemmer et al., 2000) to define the dialog, which also provides an interface for the wizard. SUEDE defines a dialog in a state machine, in which the system prompts are states and user inputs are edges between them. The content of system prompts was synthesized with NUANCE Vocalizer Expressive[1] version 1.2.1 (Voice: anna.full). During the experiment, after each user input the wizards clicks the corresponding edge and SUEDE plays the next prompt. All user utterances are recorded as audio files.

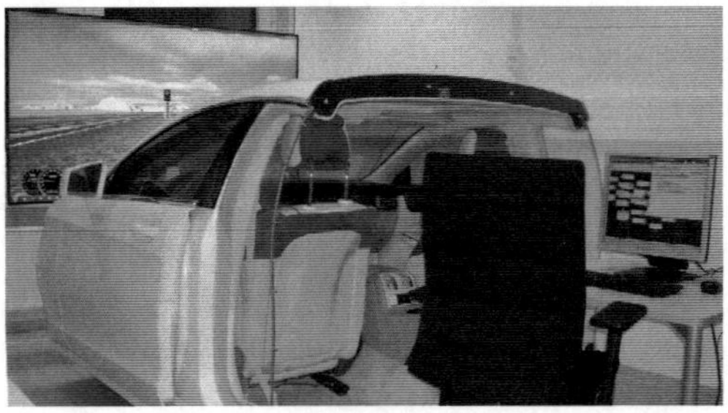

Figure 1: Experimental Set-Up

4.2 Experiment Design

Infotainment systems in cars are used while driving. This means the user cannot concentrate on the infotainment system only, but also has to focus on the road. According to multiple resource theory, the human's performance is reduced when human resources overlap (Wickens, 2008). In a dual-task scenario, like using the infotainment system while driving, multiple resources are allocated and may interfere. Considering this issue, we use a driving task to keep the participants occupied while they interact with the SDS. This allows us to observe user utterances in a stressful situation.

Infotainment systems in cars are often equipped with large displays providing visual and haptic interaction. These kinds of interaction compete for human resources which are needed for driving. This results in driver distraction, especially in demanding secondary tasks (Young and Regan, 2007). Furthermore, a visual interface can also influence the communication of users (e.g. they utter visual terms). As we intent to study how a user interacts naturally with a multi-domain SDS, we avoid priming effects by not using any visual interface.

4.2.1 Primary Task: Driving Simulator

One major requirement for the driving task is to keep the driver occupied at a constant level all the time. Otherwise, we would not be able to analyze user utterances on a fine-grained level.

[1] http://www.nuance.com/for-business/mobile-solutions/vocalizer-expressive/index.htm

Therefore, we used the **Con**tinuous **T**racking and **Re**action (ConTRe) task (Mahr et al., 2012) which allows controlled driving conditions. It consists of a steering and a reaction task, which require operating the steering wheel and pedals. In the steering task, a yellow cylinder moves unpredictable right and left at a constant distance from the driver and the driver must always steer towards it. This is similar to driving on a curved road. Sometimes a driver needs to react to sudden events to prevent an accident. For this a traffic light shows randomly red and green and requires the driver to push the throttle or brake pedal. The movement of the yellow cylinder and the appearance of the stop light can be controlled by manipulating control variables. The "hard driving setting" from Mahr et al. (2012) was used in this study.

4.2.2 Secondary Task: cross application tasks with speech interaction

As described in Section 3, a task consists of three subtasks and each subtask requires two to four semantic concepts. For a user it is possible to insert multiple concepts at once:

U: "Search an Italian restaurant at the destination"

or as single utterances in a dialog:

U: "Search an Italian restaurant"

S: "Where do you search an Italian restaurant?"

U: "At my destination"

For all possible combinations prompts were specified. SUEDE provides a GUI for the wizard to select which semantic concept a user input contains. Dependent on the selection, either another concept is requested or the answer is provided. Furthermore, a user input can optionally contain a verb expressing what the system should do. For example, if users say "Italian Restaurant" the reaction is the same as they would say "Search an Italian restaurant".

The user has basically two options to select or switch to an application. Either an explicit selection such as:

U: "Open restaurant application"

S: "Restaurant, what do you want?"

or an implicit selection such as:

U: "Search an Italian restaurant"

By using an explicit selection, users assume they have to set the context to a specific application. After that, they can use the functionality of this application. This is a common interaction schema for visual-based infotainment systems or smartphones, as they cluster their functionality into various applications. An implicit selection is rather like current personal assistants interact, as they do not cluster their functionality. Implicit selection facilitates the interaction for users since they can get an answer right away. After the user provided the necessary input for one subtask, the system responds for example:

S: "There is one Italian restaurant: Pizzeria San Marco."

Then the user needs to initiate an application switch to proceed with his task.

A system enabling user-initiated dialogs cannot always understand the user correctly. Especially in implicit selection, the language models increase, and thus recognition as well as understanding is error prone (Carstensen et al., 2010). Furthermore, the user could request a functionality which is not supported by the system. Therefore, error handling strategies need to be applied. In terms of miscommunication, it can be distinguished between misunderstanding and non-understanding (Skantze, 2007). In the experiment, two of our tasks do not support an implicit application switch, but require an explicit switch. So if users try to switch implicitly, the system will not understand their input in one task and will misinterpret it in the other task. A response to misunderstanding might look like:

U: "Search an Italian restaurant"

S: "In an Italian restaurant you can eat pizza"

A non-understanding informs the user and encourages him to try another request:

S: "Action unknown, please change your request"

These two responses are used until the user changes his strategy to explicit selection. If that does not happen, the task is aborted by the wizard if the user gets too frustrated. This enables us to analyze whether users will switch their strategy or not and how many turns it will take.

4.3 Procedure

The experiment starts with an initial questionnaire to create a profile of the participant, concerning age, experience with smartphones, infotainment systems and SDSs. Then participants are introduced to the driving task and they have time to practice till being experienced. After completing a baseline drive, they start to use the SDS. For each spoken dialog task users get a story describing in prose what they like to achieve with the system. To minimize priming effects, they have to remember their task and are not allowed to keep the description during the interaction. There is no explanation or example of the SDS, apart from a start command for activation. After the start command, the system plays a beep and the user can say whatever he likes to achieve his task. The exploration phase consists of four tasks, in which users can switch applications implicitly and explicitly. Then they rate the usability of the system with the questionnaire: **S**ubjective **A**ssessment of **S**peech **S**ystem **I**nterfaces (SASSI) (Hone and Graham, 2000). In the second part of the experiment, four tasks with different interaction schemes for application switches are completed randomly: implicit & explicit switch possible, misunderstanding, non-understanding, and dialog-initiative change.

5 Dialog Data Analysis

All audio files of user utterances were transcribed and manually annotated by one person concerning the application selection/switch, speaking style, anaphoric references, and semantic concepts.

First of all, for each application entry and switch it was classified whether the participant used an implicit or explicit utterance. Additionally, the non-understanding and misunderstanding data sets were marked whether the dialog strategy was changed and how many dialog turns this took.

Since most of the user utterances were implicit ones (see Section 6.1), we classified them further into different speaking styles. In the data set of implicit utterances, five different speaking styles could be identified. Table 2 shows them with an example. The illocutionary speech act to search a hotel is always the same, but how users express their request varies. Keyword style and explicit demand is rather how we expect people to speak with machines, as these communication forms are short commands and might be regarded as impolite between humans. Kinder and gentler communications forms are implicit demands, Wh-questions, and Yes-No-Questions. This is how we would expect people to interact with each other.

Keyword Style	*"Restaurant search. Berlin"*
Implicit Demand	*"I'd like to search a restaurant in Berlin."*
Wh-Question	*"Which restaurants are in Berlin?"*
Yes-No-Question	*"Are there any restaurants in Berlin?"*
Explicit Demand	*"Search restaurants in Berlin"*

Table 2: Speaking styles of user utterances.

Two applications are always linked with a common semantic concept. The user has to refer to this concept which he can do in various ways with anaphoric expressions. The annotation of the data set is based on Fromkin et al. (2003) and shown in Table 3 (Examples are user utterances in response to the system prompt "Navigation to Berlin started"). In an elliptic anaphoric reference the concept is not spoken, but still understood because of context - also called gapping. Furthermore, pronominalization can be used as an anaphor. We distinguish between a pronoun or adverb anaphor and an anaphor with a definite noun phrase, since the later contains the type of semantic concept. Another way is simply to rephrase the semantic concept.

Elliptic	*"Search restaurants."*
Pronoun, Adverb	*"Search restaurants there."*
Definite Noun Phrase	*"Search restaurants in this city."*
Rephrase	*"Search restaurants in Berlin."*

Table 3: Anaphoric reference types.

6 Results

In the following, results on application awareness, speaking style, anaphoric expressions, efficiency, and usability are presented. We analyzed data from 31 participants (16m/15f), with average age of 26.65 (SD: 3.32). 26 people possess and use a smartphone on a regular basis and 25 of them are used to application-based interaction (18 people use 1-5 apps and 7 people use 6-10 apps each day). Their experience with SDS is little (6-Likert Scale, avg: 3.06, SD: 1.48) as well as the usage of SDSs (5-Likert Scale, avg: 2.04, SD: 1.16). We asked them how they usually approach a new system or app to learn its interaction schema and scope of operation. On the smartphone, all 31 of them try a new app without informing themselves how it is used. Concerning infotainment systems, trying is also the most used learning approach, even while driving (26 people). This means, people do not read a manual, but the system has to be naturally usable.

In total, we built a corpus of interactions with 5h 25min with 3h 08min of user speech. It contains 243 task entries and 444 subtask switches. Due to data loss 5 task entries could not be analyzed. Subtask switches were less than theoretically possible, because misunderstanding and non-understanding tasks were aborted by the wizard if the user did not change his strategy. Concerning the type of subtask, we analyzed 91 action and 152 information seeking subtasks for task entries, as well as

236 actions and 208 information seekings for task switches.

6.1 Application Awareness

The SDS was designed to be strictly user-initiative: after a beep users could say whatever they liked. We counted 4.9% of user utterances as explicit entries to start a task, which means users in general assume either the SDS is already in the right application context or it is not based on different applications. This is an interaction schema which would rather be used with a human communication partner. 1.1% explicit utterances in subtask switches reinforce this assumption. Utterances addressing more than one application could not be observed.

Furthermore, we analyzed whether users change their strategy from implicit to explicit subtask switch if the system does not react as expected. The implicit switch was prevented and the system answered as if a misunderstanding or a non-understanding has occurred. Table 4 shows results for the number of subtask switches (subt. sw.), number of successful strategy changes (succ.), and average number of user utterances (avg. UDT) till the strategy was changed. In total, only in 43.7% subtask switches users changed their strategy. The difference between non-understanding and misunderstanding was not significant (p=0.051), however, this might due to small sample size.

	subt. sw.	**succ.**	**avg. UDT**
non-underst.	42	15	2.93 (SD=1.91)
misunderst.	45	23	3.74 (SD=1.79)

Table 4: Dialog repair changes to explicit strategy.

In summary, only 6% of user utterances addressed the application explicitly and only 43.7% of users changed their strategy from implicit to explicit. These results reveal that most users are not aware of different applications or do not address applications differently in a speech-only infotainment system. They interact rather like with a human being or with a personal assistant than with a typical in-car SDS.

6.2 Speaking styles of implicit application selection

Even if people interact without being aware of different applications, they might speak to a system in another way than to a human. We analyzed the implicit user utterances according to different speaking styles (see Figure 2). Overall, explicit demand dominates with 37.07% for task entry and 42.42% for subtask switching. Keyword style is used in 16.16% for task entry and 9.29% for subtask switches. As mentioned, explicit demand and keyword style are rather used in human-computer interaction. Here, slightly more than half of the participants (entry: 53.23%; switch: 51.71%) use this kind of interaction. The other half interacts in kinder and gentler forms known from human-human communication.

Comparing task entry and subtask switch, differences could be found in keyword style, implicit demand, and Yes-No-Question. In the first contact with the system, users might be unsure what it is capable of, therefore, often keywords were used to find out how the system reacts. Additionally, the task description was formulated in implicit demand style, thus an unsure user might remember this sentence and use it. Concerning the Yes-No-Questions, they might be a reaction to the naturally formulated system prompts, thus the user adapts to a human-human-like communication style.

Finally, we compare information seeking subtasks with action subtasks. In action subtasks, implicit and explicit demand style dominate. This is reasonable, as people give commands in either form and expect a system reaction. Likewise, it was anticipated that question styles are used for information seeking. One interesting finding is that keyword style is more often used in information seeking. This could be due to priming effects of using search engines like Google[2], in which users only insert the terms they are interested in and Google provides the most likely answers.

In summary, speaking styles vary. Sometimes the system is considered as a human-like communication partner and sometimes users try to reach their goal as fast as possible by giving short commands. However, speaking styles depend on the type of subtask and dialog state.

6.3 Anaphoric Expressions

In a cross-application task, it is of interest how users refer to application-linking semantic concepts. Figure 3 shows which kind of anaphoric expressions were used in implicit utterances. Nearly half of the utterances (47.68%) contain a rephrase of the semantic concept and further 31.57% a def-

[2]www.google.de

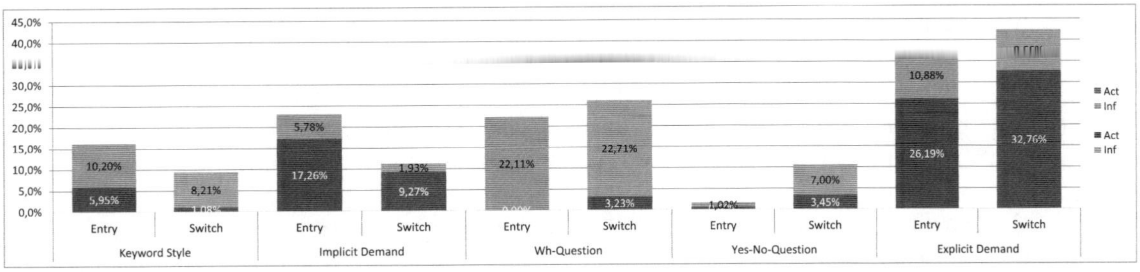

Figure 2: Speaking styles of implicit task entry and subtask switch distinguished by action (Act) and information seeking (Inf)

inite noun phrase. A rephrase utterance can be interpreted easily for an SDS, since there is no need to determine the right antecedent from dialog history. A definite noun phrase contains the semantic type of the antecedent and can be refered easily in a semantic annotated dialog history. However, a pronoun or elliptic anaphoric expression is harder to resolve, as the former only describes the syntactic form of the antecedent and the later does not contain any information of the antecedent. Sometimes, also humans are not able to resolve an anaphoric expression easily. Comparing information seeking and action subtasks, the only difference can be identified between definite noun phrases and rephrase. In information seeking subtasks, participants rephrased more often than using definite noun phrases.

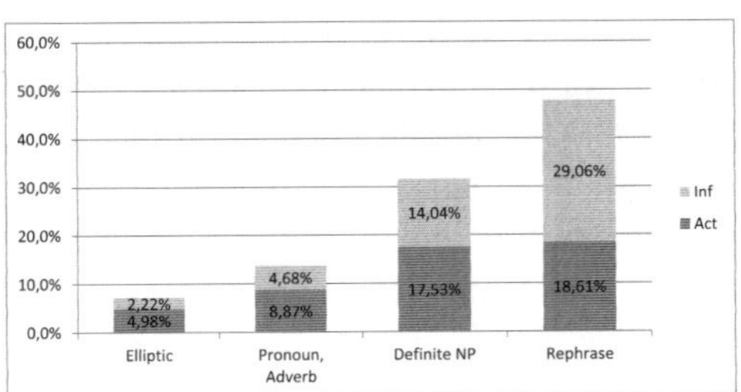

Figure 3: Anaphoric expressions used in implicit application switches.

6.4 Efficiency

Especially in the car it is essential to support short and efficient interactions. In this study, participants used on average 6.27 (SD: 2.62) words for one utterance. However, the word length of a user utterance is only one part which influences dialog length. The number of semantic concepts uttered is more important, as the more semantic concepts are spoken, the less system prompts are needed to request missing information. The semantic concepts of each user utterance were annotated and counted (avg: 2.77; SD: 0.73; min: 1; max: 6). They are set in relation to the maximum required semantic concepts (avg: 3.26; SD: 0.59; min: 2; max: 4) for the corresponding subtask. We divide the spoken concepts by the maximum concepts to calculate an efficiency score (avg: 0.86; SD: 0.22). This means 86% of user utterances contain all necessary semantic concepts to answer the request. Therefore, in-car SDS need to understand multiple semantic concepts in one utterance to keep a dialog short, such as the city, street and street number for a destination entry.

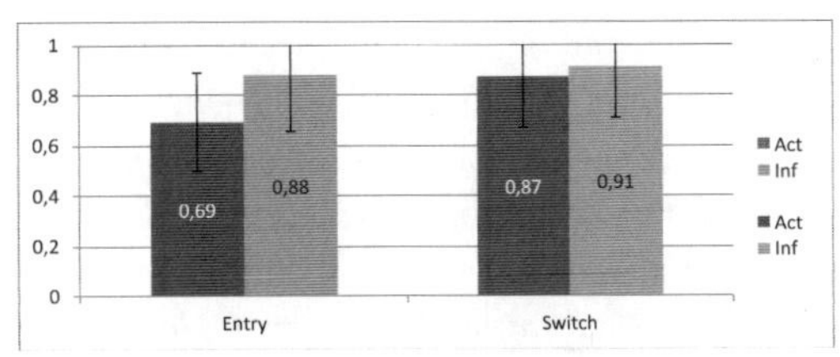

Figure 4: Efficiency scores of user utterances.

Figure 4 shows efficiency scores split into task entry and subtask switch as well as action and information seeking. In total, there is no significant difference between task entry and subtask switch concerning number of words, semantic concepts, or efficiency score. Comparing types of subtasks at task entry, the efficiency score for action subtasks (avg: 0.69; SD: 0.2) is significantly ($p=0.0018$) less than for information seeking subtasks (avg. 0.88; SD 0.22). Although, significantly ($p=0.0003$) more semantic concepts in actions were required (avg: 3.66; SD: 0.48) than in information seekings (avg: 3.2; SD: 0.4), users do not utter more semantic concepts. How many semantic concepts users can utter in one sentence while driving, needs to be addressed in the future.

6.5 Usability

Usability is a necessary condition in order to evaluate if people will use a system. The SASSI scores provide valid evidence of a system's usability. Figure 5 shows results separated into the six dimensions System Response Accuracy (SRA), Likeability (Like), Cognitive Demand (Cog Dem), Annoyance (Ann), Habitability (Hab), and Speed. A 7-Likert scale was used and recoded to values [-3, ..., 3]. If a system is less annoying, its usability will be better. Thus, except of cognitive demand and habitability, the usability of our SDS is rated good. The low habitability score is due to the fact that we did not explain the SDS and after four tasks users are not completely accustomed to the system.

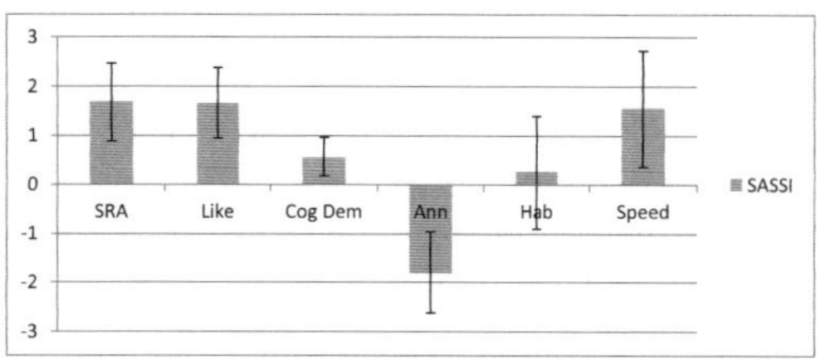

Figure 5: SASSI Usability scores.

7 Discussion and Further Research

The results show, that users are in general not aware of different applications in speech-only in-car SDSs and switch implicitly between different domains. This interaction schema is similar to human-human communication, but may differ if the user is primed through a visual representation. Concerning speaking styles, more than half of the participants used keyword style and explicit demand, which might be regarded impolite between humans. They are aware to communicate with a system lacking emotions. A user, who is not sure about the system's functions, will rather start with keywords and, after hearing natural formulated system prompts, is likely to adapt to natural speaking styles. A human-like prompt (instead of our beep) may ensure the user from the beginning. Obviously, speaking styles depend on type of task, thus question and keyword style is used for information seeking and demand style to initiate an action. More than 50% of the participants used anaphoric expressions, which have to be resolved within dialog context. This is comprehensible, as for people it is usually easier and more efficient to pronounce an anaphor than to pronounce the antecedent. For reaching their interaction goal fast and efficient, the participants used multiple semantic concepts in utterances. In total, 86% of user utterances contain all necessary information to answer the request. This results in less dialog turns and thus is fundamental for in-car systems. In addition, the usability is rated good, thus the system might be accepted by drivers.

Another crucial point for in-car systems is that they should distract the driver as little as possible. It can be assumed that without visual and haptic distractions, the driver would keep his focus on the road. However, cognitive demand also causes distraction. The moderate SASSI score for cognitive demand requires an objective test. Therefore, we will analyze multi-domain interactions with respect to mental pressure and driver performance for further research. So far, we have only considered multi-domain dialogs with one common semantic concept. By referring to multiple semantic concepts, drivers might use more anaphoric expressions or aggregate them with a general term, which needs to be address in further experiments.

8 Conclusions

This paper presents results on how young and technically affine people interact with in-car SDSs in performing multi-domain tasks. 31 participants completed all together 243 tasks (each with two application switches) while driving in a fixed-base driving simulator. In this experiment, a controlled WoZ setup was used instead of a real speech recognition system.

The results identify important guidelines for multi-domain SDSs. Since users are in general not aware of applications in speech-only dialog systems, implicit application switching is required. However, this should not replace explicit switching commands. Speaking styles vary and depend on type of task, and dialog state. Thus language models must therefore consider this issue. People rely on anaphora, which means an SDS must maintain a extensive dialog history across multiple applications to enable coreference resolution. It is further necessary that the SDS supports multiple semantic concepts in one utterance since it enables an efficient interaction and drivers use this. The SDS's usability was rated good by the participants. For further research, we will analyze multi-domain interaction with respect to driver performance and multiple semantic concept anaphora.

Acknowledgments

The work presented here was funded by GetHomeSafe (EU 7th Framework STREP 288667).

References

Kai-Uwe Carstensen, Christian Ebert, Cornelia Ebert, Susanne Jekat, Ralf Klabunde, and Hagen Langer. 2010. *Computerlinguistik und Sprachtechnologie*. Spektrum, Akad. Verl.

Hua Cheng, Harry Bratt, Rohit Mishra, Elizabeth Shriberg, Sandra Upson, Joyce Chen, Fuliang Weng, Stanley Peters, Lawrence Cavedon, and John Niekrasz. 2004. A wizard of oz framework for collecting spoken human-computer dialogs. In *Proc. of ICSLP-2000*.

Victor Ei-Wen Lo and Paul A. Green. 2013. Development and evaluation of automotive speech interfaces: Useful information from the human factors and the related literature. *Int. Journal of Vehicular Technology*, 2013:13.

Norman M. Fraser and G.Nigel Gilbert. 1991. Simulating speech systems. *Computer Speech & Language*, 5(1):81 – 99.

Victoria Fromkin, Robert Rodman, and Nina Hyams. 2003. *An Introduction to Language*. Rosenberg, Michael, 7 edition.

Petra Geutner, Frank Steffens, and Dietrich Manstetten. 2002. Design of the vico spoken dialogue system: Evaluation of user expectations by wizard-of-oz experiments. In *Proc. of the Int. Conf. on Language Resources and Evaluation*, volume 2.

James Glass, Joseph Polifroni, Stephanie Seneff, and Victor Zue. 2000. Data collection and performance evaluation of spoken dialogue systems: The mit experience. In *Proc. of 6th INT*.

Hansjörg Hofmann, Ute Ehrlich, André Berton, and Wolfgang Minker. 2012. Speech interaction with the internet - a user study. In *Intelligent Environments*, Guanajuato, Mexico.

Kate S Hone and Robert Graham. 2000. Towards a tool for the subjective assessment of speech system interfaces (sassi). *Natural Language Engineering*, 6(3&4):287–303.

Melanie Kellar, Carolyn Watters, and Michael Shepherd. 2006. A goal-based classification of web information tasks. In *In 69th Annual Meeting of the American Society for Information Science and Technology (ASIST)*.

Scott R. Klemmer, Anoop K. Sinha, Jack Chen, James A. Landay, Nadeem Aboobaker, and Annie Wang. 2000. Suede: a wizard of oz prototyping tool for speech user interfaces. In *Proc. of the 13th annual ACM symposium on User interface software and technology*, New York. ACM.

Jannette Maciej and Mark Vollrath. 2009. Comparison of manual vs. speech-based interaction with in-vehicle information systems. *Accident Analysis and Prevention*, 41(5):924 – 930.

Angela Mahr, Michael Feld, Mohammad Mehdi Moniri, and Rafael Math. 2012. The contre (continuous tracking and reaction) task: A flexible approach for assessing driver cognitive workload with high sensitivity. In Andrew L. Kun, Linda Ng Boyle, Bryan Reimer, and Andreas Riener, editors, *Adj. Proc. of the 4th International Conference on Automotive User Interfaces and Interactive Vehicular Applications*, Portsmouth. ACM.

National Highway Traffic Safety Administration (NHTSA). 2013. Distracted driving 2011. Technical report.

Norbert Reithinger, Jan Alexandersson, Tilman Becker, Anselm Blocher, Ralf Engel, Markus Löckelt, Jochen Müller, Norbert Pfleger, Peter Poller, Michael Streit, and Valentin Tschernomas. 2003. Smartkom: Adaptive and flexible multimodal access to multiple applications. In *Multimodal interfaces*, New York.

Gabriel Skantze. 2007. *Error Handling in Spoken Dialogue Systems*. Ph.D. thesis, KTH Computer Science and Communication.

Jessica Villing, Cecilia Holtelius, Staffan Larsson, Anders Lindstrm, Alexander Seward, and Nina berg. 2008. Interruption, resumption and domain switching in in-vehicle dialogue. In Bengt Nordstrm and Aarne Ranta, editors, *Advances in Natural Language Processing*, volume 5221 of *Lecture Notes in Computer Science*, pages 488–499. Springer Berlin Heidelberg.

Fuliang Weng, Baoshi Yan, Zhe Feng, Florin Ratiu, Madhuri Raya, Brian Lathrop, Annie Lien, Sebastian Varges, Rohit Mishra, Feng Lin, Matthew Purver, Harry Bratt, Yao Meng, Stanley Peters, Tobias Scheideck, Badri Raghunathan, and Zhaoxia Zhang. 2007. Chat to your destination. In *Proc. of 8th SIGdial Workshop on Discourse and Dialogue*.

Christopher D Wickens. 2008. Multiple resources and mental workload. In *Human factors*, volume 50, pages 449–55. USA.

Kristie Young and Michael Regan. 2007. Driver distraction: A review of the literature. *Distracted Driving*, pages 379–405.

IBM's Belief Tracker: Results On Dialog State Tracking Challenge Datasets

Rudolf Kadlec, Jindřich Libovický, Jan Macek, and Jan Kleindienst
IBM Czech Republic
V Parku 4, Prague 4
Czech Republic
{rudolf_kadlec, jindrich_libovicky, jmacek2, jankle}@cz.ibm.com

Abstract

Accurate dialog state tracking is crucial for the design of an efficient spoken dialog system. Until recently, quantitative comparison of different state tracking methods was difficult. However the 2013 Dialog State Tracking Challenge (DSTC) introduced a common dataset and metrics that allow to evaluate the performance of trackers on a standardized task. In this paper we present our belief tracker based on the Hidden Information State (HIS) model with an adjusted user model component. Further, we report the results of our tracker on test3 dataset from DSTC. Our tracker is competitive with trackers submitted to DSTC, even without training it achieves the best results in L2 metrics and it performs between second and third place in accuracy. After adjusting the tracker using the provided data it outperformed the other submissions also in accuracy and yet improved in L2. Additionally we present preliminary results on another two datasets, test1 and test2, used in the DSTC. Strong performance in L2 metric means that our tracker produces well calibrated hypotheses probabilities.

1 Introduction

Spoken dialog systems need to keep a representation of the dialog state and the user goal to follow an efficient interaction path. The performance of state-of-the-art speech recognition systems varies widely with domain and environment with word accuracy rates ranging from less than 70% to 98%, which often leads to misinterpretation of the user's intention. Dialog state tracking methods need to cope with such error-prone automatic speech recognition (ASR) and spoken language understanding (SLU) outputs. Traditional dialog systems use hand-crafted rules to select from the SLU outputs based on their confidence scores. Recently, several data-driven approaches to dialog state tracking were developed as a part of end-to-end spoken dialog systems. However, specifics of these systems render comparison of dialog state tracking methods difficult.

The Dialog State Tracking Challenge (DSTC) (Williams et al., 2013) provides a shared testbed with datasets and tools for evaluation of dialog state tracking methods. It abstracts from subsystems of end-to-end spoken dialog systems focusing only on the dialog state estimation and tracking. It does so by providing datasets of ASR and SLU outputs with reference transcriptions together with annotation on the level of dialog acts.

In this paper we report initial encouraging results of our generative belief state tracker. We plan to investigate discriminative approaches in the future.

The rest of the paper continues as follows. In the next section we formally introduce the dialog tracking task together with datasets used in the DSTC. Then in Section 3 we discuss related work. Section 4 describes the belief update equations of our tracker. After that we introduce the design of our whole tracking system, especially how we trained the system in a supervised setting on the train dataset and in an unsupervised setting on the test dataset. In Section 6 we show results of our trackers, compare them to other DSTC participants, and discuss the results in the context of design choices and task characteristics.

2 DSTC Problem Definition, Datasets and Metrics

The task of the DSTC can be formally defined as computing $\mathsf{P}(g_t|\mathbf{u}_{0:t}, a_{0:t})$. That is, for each time step t of the dialog compute the probability distribution over the user's hidden goal g given a sequence of SLU hypotheses from the

Dataset	System	#	Annotated
train1a	A	1013	yes
train1b	A	1117	no
train1c	A	9502	no
train2	A	643	yes
train3	B	688	yes
test1	A	715	for eval. only
test2	A	750	for eval. only
test3	B	1020	for eval. only
test4	C	438	for eval. only

Table 1: Datasets description. The *System* column shows what dialog system was used to collect the dataset. The # column shows the number of dialogs in the dataset. The last column informs whether the ground truth annotation was provided with the dataset.

System	Dial. model	SLU scores
A	open	$\langle -\inf, 0\rangle$
B	fixed	$\langle 0, 1\rangle$
C	open	$\langle 0, 1\rangle$

Table 2: Main features of the dialog managers used to collect the datasets. System A and C use open dialog structure where the user can respond with any combination of slots on any machine question. System B uses a fixed dialog structure where the user can respond only with the concept the system expects.

beginning of the dialog up to the time t denoted as $\mathbf{u}_{0:t}$ and a sequence of machine actions $a_{0:t}$. It is assumed that the goal is fixed through the dialog, unless the user is informed that the requested goal does not exist. In DSTC the user's goal consist of nine slots: *route, from.desc, from.neighborhood, from.monument, to.desc, to.neighborhood, to.monument, date, time*.

The dialog datasets in the DSTC are partitioned into five training sets and four test sets. Details and differences of the datasets are summarized in Table 1 and 2. The datasets come from dialog systems deployed by three teams denoted as A, B and C. All the training datasets were transcribed but only three of them were annotated on the level of dialog acts. The SLU confidence scores from system B are relatively well calibrated, meaning that confidences can be directly interpreted as probabilities of observing the SLU hypothesis. Confidence scores from the system A are not well calibrated as noted by several DSTC participants (Lee and Eskenazi, 2013; Kim et al., 2013).

The evaluation protocol is briefly described in Section 6. Its detailed description can be found in (Williams et al., 2012), its evaluation in (Williams et al., 2013).

In 2013, nine teams with 27 trackers participated in the challenge. The results of the best trackers will be discussed together with the results of our tracker later in Section 6.

3 Related Work

This section shortly reviews current approaches to dialog state tracking. We divide the trackers into two broad families of generative and discriminative methods.

3.1 Generative Methods

The HIS model (Young et al., 2010) introduces an approximative method of solving the belief tracking as an inference in a dynamic Bayesian network with SLU hypotheses and machine actions as observed variables and the estimate of the user's goal as a hidden variable. The HIS model was implemented several times (Williams, 2010; Gašić, 2011). Recent criticism of generative methods for belief tracking brought more attention to the discriminative methods (Williams, 2012b).

In the DSTC only few generative system participated. Kim et al. (2013) implemented the HIS model with additional discriminative rescoring, Wang and Lemon (2013) introduced a very simple model based on hand-crafted rules. Both of them scored between the second and the fourth place in the challenge.

3.2 Discriminative Methods

As was previously mentioned, the discriminative methods received more attention recently.

The overall winner of the DSTC (Lee and Eskenazi, 2013) used a maximum entropy model, which they claim to be outperformed by bringing more structure to the model by using the Conditional Random Fields (Lee, 2013). The same type of model is used also by Ren et al. (2013). Usage of Deep Neural Networks was tested by Henderson et al. (2013).

Žilka et al. (2013) compare a discriminative maximum entropy model and a generative method based on approximate inference in a Bayesian network, with the discriminative model preforming better.

4 Model

Our model is an implementation of the HIS model (Young et al., 2010). In HIS the belief state is viewed as a probability distribution over all possible user's goals. The belief state is represented by a set of so-called *partitions*, which are sets of user's goals that are indistinguishable based on actions the system observes. It means the probability mass assigned to a partition spreads to the user's goals in the partition proportionally to their's prior probabilities. The belief update is performed in two steps.

Belief refinement ensures that for each user action on the SLU n-best list and each partition all goals in the partition are either consistent with the user action or not. This step does not change the belief state, it only enables the actual belief update to be computed using the update equation (Eq. 1).

The partitions are organized in a tree structure for which it holds that a child and a parent partition are identical in some slots and complementary in the remaining ones. This is ensured by the belief refinement procedure. For each observed user action and each partition it first checks whether all of the hypotheses in the partition are either consistent with the action or not. If they are not, it splits the partition into two partitions with the parent-child relationship. The inconsistent hypotheses remain in the parent partition and the consistent ones are moved to the child. The belief of the original partition is distributed between the new ones in the ratio of their priors.

To prevent an exponential increase in the number of partitions during the dialog, a partition recombination strategy can be used that removes the less probable partition and moves their hypotheses to different partitions. We perform partition recombination at the end of each turn (Henderson and Lemon, 2008), during the recombination low probability partitions are merged with their parents exactly as suggested by Williams (2010).

For the actual belief update the following standard update equation is used:

$$\mathsf{P}_{t+1}(p) = k \cdot \mathsf{P}_t(p) \cdot \sum_{u \in \mathbf{u}} \mathsf{P}(u|\mathbf{u}) \cdot \mathsf{P}(u|p,a) \quad (1)$$

where k is a normalization constant, $\mathsf{P}_t(p)$ is belief in partition p after turn t, a is the machine action taken in turn t, $\mathbf{u}$ is a set of observed user actions, $\mathsf{P}(u|\mathbf{u})$ is the score of action u in the SLU n-best list $\mathbf{u}$. In this definition $\mathsf{P}_0(p)$ is a prior probability of partition p; the prior might be either uniform or estimated from the training data. The list $\mathbf{u}$ is extended with an unobserved action $\tilde{u}$ whose probability is:

$$\mathsf{P}(\tilde{u}|\mathbf{u}) = 1 - \sum_{u \in \mathbf{u} \setminus \{\tilde{u}\}} \mathsf{P}(u|\mathbf{u}). \quad (2)$$

$\mathsf{P}(u|p,a)$ in the update equation is the *user model*, i.e. how likely the user is to take an action u given that the last machine action was a and user's goal is represented by partition p.

In our case:

$$\mathsf{P}(u|p,a) = \frac{\Lambda(p,u,a)}{\sum_{p' \in \text{partitions}} \Lambda(p',u,a) \cdot \text{size}(p')} \quad (3)$$

where $\text{size}(p)$ is the number of possible user's goals represented by p and $\Lambda(p,u,a)$ is an indicator function that evaluates to 1 when user's action u is compatible with the goal represented by p given the last machine's action was a, otherwise Λ evaluates to 0.

Λ is defined in the following way, for every observed action $u \in \mathbf{u} \setminus \{\tilde{u}\}$:

$$\Lambda(p,u,a) = \Lambda'(p,u,a) \quad (4)$$

where Λ' is a deterministic function that encodes the meanings of user and machine actions for a given partition. The rules expressed by Λ' are for example:

$$\forall a : \Lambda'(p_{s=w}, \mathit{inform}(s=v), a) = \begin{cases} 1 & \text{if } v = w \\ 0 & \text{if } v \neq w \end{cases}$$

and

$$\Lambda'(p_{s=w}, \mathit{yes}(), \mathit{conf}(s=v)) = \begin{cases} 1 & \text{if } v = w \\ 0 & \text{if } v \neq w \end{cases}$$

where $p_{s=w}$ represents a partition where slot s has value w, $\mathit{inform}(s=v)$ is user's action assigning value v to the slot s and $\mathit{conf}(s=v)$ is machine action requiring confirmation that slot s has value v.

For an unobserved action $\tilde{u}$ we define Λ as:

$$\Lambda(p,\tilde{u},a) = \prod_{u \in \mathbf{u} \setminus \{\tilde{u}\}} (1 - \Lambda'(p,u,a)). \quad (5)$$

This definition assumes that user's unobserved action $\tilde{u}$ uniformly supports each partition not supported by any of the observed user's actions u. $\Lambda(p, \tilde{u}, a)$ evaluates to 1 if none of user's actions support given partition, otherwise it evaluates to 0. This can be viewed as an axiom of our system, alternatively we could assume that $\tilde{u}$ supports all partitions, not only those not supported by any observed action.

The key property of the update equations formulated in this way is that the probability of a partition representing a hypothesis that a user's goal was not mentioned in any of the SLU lists up to the time t does not outweigh probability of observed goals even though the prior probability of unobserved hypothesis is usually orders of magnitude higher than the probability of all observed hypotheses. However, when two goals are indistinguishable based on the SLU input then the ratio of their probabilities will be exactly the ratio of their priors.

Belief update equations are generic and independent of the internal structure of partitions. When the tracker has to be adapted to a new dialog domain with the fixed goal the application developer needs to supply only a new definition of Λ' and partition splitting mechanism adjusted according to Λ'.

4.1 Differences to the Original HIS

The key difference between our HIS implementation and previous HIS systems is in the formulation of the user model. Previous HIS-based systems (Young et al., 2010; Gašić, 2011) factorize the user model as:

$$\mathsf{P}^{orig}(u|p, a) = k \cdot \mathsf{P}(\mathcal{T}(u)|\mathcal{T}(a)) \cdot \mathcal{M}(u, p, a)$$

where $\mathsf{P}(\mathcal{T}(u)|\mathcal{T}(a))$ is a dialog act type bigram model and $\mathcal{M}$ is a deterministic item matching model that is similar to our Λ. Based on a description of the item matching model given in (Keizer et al., 2008; Young et al., 2010; Gašić, 2011) we deduce that it evaluates to a constant c_+ instead of 1 when the user action is consistent with the partition and to c_- instead of 0 otherwise. It holds that $0 \leq c_- \ll c_+ \leq 1$, e.g. $c_- = 0.1$ and $c_+ = 0.9$.

In our tracker, we omit the dialog act type model since it is not a mandatory component of the user model and it can be added later. However, the most important systematic difference between our tracker and the original HIS formulation is that instead of using a reduced user model, which would be $\mathsf{P}^{orig}(u|p, a) = \Lambda(p, u, a)$ in the original HIS, we use the formulation given in Eq. 3. The original HIS does not use a concept of partition's size (size(p') in Eq. 3) that we need for the definition of our user model.

Par.	P_t	P_{t+1}^{orig}	P_{t+1}^{ours}
p_a	$1/3$	$1/3$	$1/4$
p_b	$1/3$	$1/3$	$1/4$
p_c	$1/3$	$1/3$	$1/2$

Table 3: Comparison of the effects of original HIS user model and our modified user model. Initially all partitions are equally likely. After performing belief update using Eq. 1 the original model outputs probabilities in the column P_{t+1}^{orig}, the column P_{t+1}^{orig} shows results of our user model.

We will illustrate the difference between these two approaches on a minimalistic abstract example. Suppose the belief space consists of three partitions p_a, p_b and p_c, each of them having probability of $1/3$ and representing one possible user's goal (i.e. size(p_*) $= 1$). There are two actions on the SLU list: $u_{a,b}$ that is consistent only with p_a and p_b (i.e. $\Lambda'(p_a, u_{a,b}, *) = 1$), and u_c that is consistent only with p_c. Both $u_{a,b}$ and u_c are equally probable, $\mathsf{P}(u_{a,b}|\mathbf{u}) = \mathsf{P}(u_c|\mathbf{u}) = 1/2$. According to one intuition p_a and p_b should *share* support given to them by action $u_{a,b}$, on the other hand p_c does not share the action u_c with any other partition. Thus after updating the probability using Eq. 1 one would expect $\mathsf{P}_{t+1}(p_c)$ to be higher than $\mathsf{P}_{t+1}(p_a)$. Now we can compare the output of our model and the original HIS side by side as shown in Table 3. The user model as formulated in the original HIS leads to a new belief state where all partitions are equally probable. However, according to our modified user model partition p_c is twice as probable than p_a or p_b. This is, we argue, closer to human intuition.

The update equation for a partition p in this simplistic example is:

$$\mathsf{P}_{t+1}(p) = k \cdot \mathsf{P}(p) \cdot \big(\mathsf{P}(u_{a,b}|\mathbf{u}) \cdot \mathsf{P}(u_{a,b}|p, *) + \mathsf{P}(u_c|\mathbf{u}) \cdot \mathsf{P}(u_c|p, *)\big).$$

For every partition the original model would output the same probability:

$$\mathsf{P}_{t+1}^{orig}(p) = k_1 \frac{1}{3}\left(\frac{1}{2} \cdot c_+ + \frac{1}{2} \cdot c_-\right) = \frac{1}{3}$$

However our model gives the following equation for both p_a and p_b:

$$\mathsf{P}_{t+1}^{our}(p_x) = k_2\,\frac{1}{3}\left(\frac{1}{2}\cdot\frac{1}{1+1}+\frac{1}{2}\cdot\frac{0}{1}\right)=\frac{1}{4}$$

where $x \in \{a, b\}$. The impact of $u_{a,b}$ on p_x is divided by a factor of 2 since it is shared by two partitions each representing one possible user goal. For p_c we have:

$$\mathsf{P}_{t+1}^{our}(p_c) = k_2\,\frac{1}{3}\left(\frac{1}{2}\cdot\frac{0}{1+1}+\frac{1}{2}\cdot\frac{1}{1}\right)=\frac{1}{2}.$$

This is how values in Table 3 were computed.

Another extension of the original HIS is how we handle the unobserved action. To our knowledge, the original HIS systems (Young et al., 2010; Gašić, 2011) do not deal with probability of unobserved action; Williams (2010) presents a different way of handling the unobserved action. We provide unified way how to handle unrecognized mass on the SLU list. In the original HIS model, partition p_{unobs} not supported by any of the observed actions obtains probability by $\mathcal{M}$ evaluating to c_{-} on each observed action. In our model, p_{unobs} receives non-zero probability due to $\Lambda(p_{unobs}, \tilde{u}, *)$ evaluating to 1 (see Eq. 5).

5 Tracker Design and its Variants

The previous section gave detailed description of the update equations of our HIS based tracker. This section presents an overall design of different implemented tracker variants. We will discuss how we use the bus route database and how we perform supervised and unsupervised prior adaptation.

5.1 Single Slot Tracking versus Joint Tracking of Multiple Slots

An advantage of a HIS-based systems is that they make it possible to track a joint probability distribution over a user's goal. This advantage is twofold. First, it enables usage of a joint prior, either learned from training data or from the bus schedule database. Second, tracking a joint distribution makes it possible to use more information from SLU hypotheses. We will illustrate this on an example. Suppose that SLU is able to extract multiple slots from one user's utterance, in our example it might be interpreted as:

```
inform(route=61,to.desc=cmu)   0.5
inform(route=60,to.desc=zoo)   0.4
```

And the machine explicitly confirms the route:

```
expl-confirm(route=61)
```

If the user's response is interpreted as:

```
negate()    0.8
affirm()    0.1
```

Then the system tracking only marginal probabilities over single slots will correctly consider route `60` as being more probable but user's negation will have no effect on marginal distribution of `to.desc`. However, a system tracking the joint distribution will now correctly rank `zoo` higher than `cmu`. The disadvantage of tracking joint hypotheses is that it requires more computational resources. A tracker tracking all slots independently with a uniform prior is denoted as $\mathrm{IBM}_{uniform}^{indep}$, a tracker tracking joint hypotheses with a uniform prior as $\mathrm{IBM}_{uniform}^{jointly}$.

5.2 Bus Schedule Database

Along with the dialog dataset DSTC organizers provided a database with bus schedules for routes in Pittsburgh area. We tested possibility to use relation between bus routes and bus stops that can be extracted from the database. First, we normalized bus stop names as found in the SLU hypotheses (e.g. by removing prepositions), in this way we were able to match 98 percent of bus stops found in the SLU to stops in the database.

An initial analysis of the data revealed that only around 55% of *route*, *from.desc*, *to.desc* hypotheses annotated by human annotators as a ground truth were also found in the database. This means that either callers were often asking for non-existing combinations or the database was mismatched.

Our tracker utilizing the database tracked joint hypotheses for *route*, *from.desc* and *to.desc* slots and hypotheses with combinations not found in the database were penalized. The prior of a joint partition $p_{r,f,t}$, for a route r from destination f to destination t, was computed as:

$$\mathsf{P}(p_{r,f,t}) = \mathsf{P}_{uniform}\cdot DB(r,f,t)$$

Where DB is

$$DB(r,f,t) = \begin{cases} 1 & \text{if } \langle r,f,t\rangle \in database \\ \frac{1}{c} & \text{otherwise} \end{cases}$$

where parameter c is a penalty constant for hypotheses not in the database. The value of c is estimated by parameter search on the train data. This tracker will be denoted as $\mathrm{IBM}_{db}^{jointly}$.

	Test set 3							
	Schedule 2				Schedule 3			
	joint acc.	avg. acc.	joint L2	avg. L2	joint acc.	avg. acc.	joint L2	avg. L2
Team 6 (Lee and Eskenazi, 2013)	**.558**	**.680**	**.801**	.597	**.589**	.823	.779	**.367**
Team 8 (unknown authors)	.424	.616	.845	**.559**	.408	.716	.878	.422
Team 9 (Kim et al., 2013)	.499	.657	.914	.710	.551	**.828**	.928	.461
Team 3 (Žilka et al., 2013)	.464	.645	.831	.669	.528	.794	**.734**	.390
1-best baseline	.448	.620	.865	.611	.492	.703	.839	.514
$\text{IBM}^{jointly}_{uniform}$	.521	.654	**.785**	.575	.557	.804	.746	**.344**
$\text{IBM}^{indep}_{uniform}$	.521	.654	**.786**	.576	.558	.806	.746	**.343**
$\text{IBM}^{jointly}_{db}$	.523	.657	**.774**	.564	.559	.806	.738	**.339**
$\text{IBM}^{indep}_{train\text{-}to\text{-}test}$	**.563**	**.680**	**.694**	**.513**	**.609**	**.828**	**.644**	**.285**
$\text{IBM}^{indep}_{unsup}$	**.573**	**.689**	**.685**	**.505**	**.611**	**.834**	**.634**	**.279**

Table 4: Results on the DSTC test set 3. Higher accuracy is better, whereas lower L2 score is better. Numbers in bold highlight performance of the best tracker in the selected metric. The first four rows show teams that performed the best in at least one of the selected metrics. For each team in each metric we show performance of the best submitted tracker. This means that numbers in one row do not have to be from a single tracker. It is an upper bound of the team's performance. The fifth row shows performance of a 1-best baseline tracker that always picks the SLU hypothesis with the top confidence. The rest are different variants of our tracker. Here the bold numbers show where our tracker performed better than the best tracker submitted to the DSTC. A light gray highlight of a cell denotes the overall best performance in online setting, a dark gray highlight denotes the best performance while tracking offline.

5.3 Priors Adaptation

We tested two variants of adjusting prior probabilities of user goals. We estimated prior probabilities as a mixture of the uniform probability and empirical distribution estimated on the training data.

In the first experiment the empirical probabilities were estimated using the annotation that was available in the training data. We tracked the slots independently because the empirical joint distribution would be too sparse to generalize on the test data. We used one prior distribution to guide the selection of *route* hypotheses Pr_{route} and one shared distribution for possible destination names Pr_{desc}. This distribution is trained on data from both *from* and *to* destinations thus gaining a more robust estimate compared to using two separate distributions for *from.desc* and *to.desc*. This tracker will be denoted as $\text{IBM}^{indep}_{train\text{-}to\text{-}test}$.

In the second experiment we used the test data without the ground truth labels to estimate the empirical prior. We first ran the tracker with the uniform prior on the testing set and we used the output hypotheses as a basis for the empirical distribution. The prior of a hypothesis is proportional to a sum of all tracker output scores for the hypothesis. This scheme is called *unsupervised prior adaptation* by Lee and Eskenazi (2013). Note that the prior was computed on the test dataset. Thus this technique is not directly applicable to a realistic setting where the belief tracker has to produce a belief for each dialog from the test set the first time it sees it. This tracker will be called $\text{IBM}^{indep}_{unsup}$.

6 Evaluation

We evaluated all our tracker variants on the DSTC test3 dataset using the protocol designed for the challenge participants. We also present initial results of the basic $\text{IBM}^{indep}_{uniform}$ and $\text{IBM}^{jointly}_{uniform}$ trackers for test1 and test2 datasets. Several quantities were measured in three different schedules, which defines, which moments of the dialog the evaluation is performed. Here we report results for schedule 2 and 3. Schedule 2 takes into account all turns when the relevant concept appeared on user's SLU list or was mentioned by the dialog system. Schedule 3 evaluates belief at the end of the dialog, i.e. at the moment when the queried information is presented to the user.

We report accuracy, which is the ratio of dialogs where the user goal was correctly estimated, and the L2 score, which is the Euclidean distance of the vector of the resulting belief from a vector having 1 for the correct hypothesis and 0s for the others. For both of these the average values over all tracked slot is reported as well as the value for the joint hypotheses. The accuracy informs us how often the correct query to the database will be made. The L2 score tells us how well-calibrated the results are, which can be important for disambiguation and for statistical policy optimization.

6.1 Method

We used one thousand partitions as the limit for the number of tracked hypotheses. For each tracker ran on the test set 3 we used only the top five SLU hypotheses.

All parameters for mixing the empirical prior probability with uniform distribution in trackers $\mathrm{IBM}^{indep}_{train\text{-}to\text{-}test}$ and $\mathrm{IBM}^{indep}_{unsup}$ were estimated using 3-fold cross validation scheme on the training data. The best parameter setting on the training data was then used in evaluation on the test set.

	Test set 1			
	joint acc.	avg. acc.	joint L2	avg. L2
Team 6	**.364**	**.862**	**.989**	**.278**
Team 9	.225	.789	1.154	.354
Team 2	.206	.777	1.234	.409
1-best baseline	.138	.626	1.220	.530
$\mathrm{IBM}^{jointly}_{uniform}$	.332	.813	.992	.282
$\mathrm{IBM}^{indep}_{uniform}$	.331	.804	1.010	.304

Table 5: Preliminary results for schedule 3 on the DSTC test set 1 of our two trackers compared to three overall well performing teams. For teams 6 and 9 see Table 4, team 2 is (Wang and Lemon, 2013). The legend of the table is the same as in Table 4.

Even though we concentrated mainly on testing the tracker on dataset 3, we also ran it on the datasets 1 and 2. For the datasets 1 and 2 we used the single best SLU hypothesis from the live system. Such hypothesis was assigned 99% probability and the remaining 1% was left for the unobserved action. For the datasets 1 and 2 a post hoc computed SLU hypotheses are available in addition to the live data. In our experiments, using the post hoc computed SLU hypotheses with normalized confidence scores yielded worse results for our tracking systems.

	Test set 2			
	joint acc.	avg. acc.	joint L2	avg. L2
Team 6	**.526**	**.854**	**.885**	**.311**
Team 9	.268	.748	1.098	.450
Team 2	.320	.764	1.148	.470
1-best baseline	.141	.487	1.185	.648
$\mathrm{IBM}^{jointly}_{uniform}$	.431	.789	**.846**	.316
$\mathrm{IBM}^{indep}_{uniform}$	.413	.778	**.875**	.332

Table 6: Preliminary results for schedule 3 on the DSTC test set 2. For teams see Tables 4 and 5. The legend of the table is the same as in Table 4.

6.2 Results

Results of our trackers on the DSTC dataset 3 are summarized in Table 4. Preliminary results of the trackers on datasets 1 and 2 whose confidence scores are not that well calibrated are shown in Tables 5 and 6. The running time of the trackers was on average below 0.05 seconds per turn[1]. The only exception is $\mathrm{IBM}^{jointly}_{db}$ that executes plenty of database queries. Although we did not focus on the computational performance optimization most of the trackers are suitable for on-line use.

6.3 Discussion

Quantitative Comparison to DSTC Trackers. First let us discuss results of our trackers on test 3 (Table 4). Here both basic variants of the tracker $\mathrm{IBM}^{indep}_{uniform}$ and $\mathrm{IBM}^{jointly}_{uniform}$ perform almost identically. This is because test 3 uses fixed dialog flow as discussed in Section 2, minor differences in performance between $\mathrm{IBM}^{indep}_{uniform}$ and $\mathrm{IBM}^{jointly}_{uniform}$ are caused only by numerical issues. The trackers are around the third place in accuracy. In joint L2 metrics they outperform the best tracker in DSTC submitted by Team 6 (Lee and Eskenazi, 2013).

Tracker utilizing database $\mathrm{IBM}^{jointly}_{db}$ does not show any significant improvement over the same tracker without database-based prior $\mathrm{IBM}^{jointly}_{uniform}$. We hypothesize that this is because of the fact that people frequently asked for non-existing combinations of routes and stops, which were penalized for not being in the database, as discussed in Sec. 5.2.

Next follow the results of tracker $\mathrm{IBM}^{indep}_{train\text{-}to\text{-}test}$ that learns priors for single slots on training dataset and uses them while inferring user's goal on the test set. In test set 3 priors enhanced

[1]On one core of Intel Xeon CPU E3-1230 V2, 3.30GHz, with memory limitation of 1GB.

tracker's performance in all metrics and the tracker outperformed all DSTC trackers.

Interesting results were achieved by $\text{IBM}^{indep}_{unsup}$ that performed even better than the $\text{IBM}^{indep}_{train\text{-}to\text{-}test}$. It uses a prior trained on the test set by running the tracker with a uniform prior. The tracker was run for three iterations each time using output of the previous iteration as a new prior.

After running the experiments with the top 5 SLU hypotheses, we performed an experiment that investigated influence of n-best list length on the tracker's accuracy. We evaluated five system variants that received 1, 2, 3, 4 and 5 best SLU hypotheses. The overall trend was that initially performance increased as more SLU hypotheses were provided however then performance started decreasing. The 3-best variant achieved about 1.5% increase in joint accuracy compared to the 1-best. However, when using more than 3 best hypotheses, the performance slightly decreased. For instance, $\text{IBM}^{indep}_{uniform}$ using 1-best hypothesis performed comparable to the 5-best configuration. Similar behavior of generative systems assuming observation independence has already been observed in different domains (Vail et al., 2007).

Based on these results we deduce two conclusions. First, strong performance of $\text{IBM}^{indep}_{uniform}$ 1-best system compared to the 1-best baseline system suggests that the main added value of our tracker in this domain is in the aggregation of observations from multiple time steps, not in tracking multiple hypotheses from one turn. Second, we attribute the effect of decreasing accuracy to the correlation of ASR errors from consecutive dialog turns. As noted by Williams (2012b), correlated ASR errors violate the assumption of observation independence that is assumed by HIS. Extending the user model with an auto-regressive component, that is with dependence on observations from the previous time step (i.e. $\mathsf{P}(u_t|\mathbf{u_{t-1}}, p, a)$), might help to tackle this problem in generative models (Wellekens, 1987).

To summarize the results on test set 3, even without any prior adaptation on the data our tracker is competitive with the best submissions to DSTC. After incorporating prior knowledge it outperforms all submitted trackers.

On test set 1 and test set 2 (see Tables 5 and 6) the trackers perform second in accuracy. In L2 metrics the trackers are competitive with the best tracker in DSTC submitted by Team 6 and they outperform it in one out of four cases. It is interesting that our basic strategy that ignores live SLU scores performed that strong.

However, on test 1 and test 2, which make it possible to input multiple slots in one user utterance, $\text{IBM}^{jointly}_{uniform}$ outperforms $\text{IBM}^{indep}_{uniform}$, both in accuracy and L2. We hypothesize that this is because of effect of tracking joint distributions described in Section 5.1.

Qualitative Comparison to DSTC Trackers. Compared to another HIS-based system (Kim et al., 2013) participating in the DSTC, our implementation does not suffer from the problem of assigning high probability to the hypothesis that the user goal was not observed so far. This might be due to our modified user model. Therefore our implementation does not need a final transformation of belief scores as reported by Kim et al. (2013).

Additionally, our implementation does not exhibit the *forgetting* behavior as experienced by Žilka et al. (2013). Forgetting is undesirable given the validity of assumption that the user's goal remains fixed in the whole dialog, which is the case of DSTC bus schedule domains.

7 Conclusion

Although the use of generative trackers was recently criticized by Williams (2012a), our results show that at least in some metrics (e.g. L2 metrics on dataset 3) a generative tracker can outperform the best state-of-the-art discriminative tracker (Lee and Eskenazi, 2013). Even though we agree that the discriminative approach might be more promising, it seems that in general there are conditions where generative models learn faster than discriminative models (Ng and Jordan, 2001). Thus it might be beneficial to use a generative tracker for a newly deployed dialog system with only a few training dialogs available and switch to a discriminative model once enough training data from an already running system is collected. Ensemble trackers incorporating both generative and discriminative models as used by Lee and Eskenazi (2013) might also be an interesting direction for future research.

Acknowledgment

We would like to thank Jiří Havelka for his valuable comments on a draft of this paper. This work was partially funded by the GetHomeSafe project (EU 7th Framework STREP project No. 288667).

References

Milica Gašić. 2011. *Statistical Dialogue Modelling*. PhD thesis, University of Cambridge.

James Henderson and Oliver Lemon. 2008. Mixture Model POMDPs for Efficient Handling of Uncertainty in Dialogue Management. In *Proc ACL-HLT*, pages 73–76.

Matthew Henderson, Blaise Thomson, and Steve Young. 2013. Deep neural network approach for the dialog state tracking challenge. In *Proceedings of the SIGDIAL 2013 Conference*, pages 467–471, Metz, France, August. Association for Computational Linguistics.

Simon Keizer, Milica Gašić, François Mairesse, Blaise Thomson, Kai Yu, and Steve Young. 2008. Modelling user behaviour in the his-pomdp dialogue manager. In *Spoken Language Technology Workshop, 2008. SLT 2008. IEEE*, pages 121–124. IEEE.

Daejoong Kim, Jaedeug Choi Choi, Kee-Eung Kim, Jungsu Lee, and Jinho Sohn. 2013. Engineering statistical dialog state trackers: A case study on dstc. In *Proceedings of the SIGDIAL 2013 Conference*, pages 462–466, Metz, France, August. Association for Computational Linguistics.

Sungjin Lee and Maxine Eskenazi. 2013. Recipe for building robust spoken dialog state trackers: Dialog state tracking challenge system description. In *Proceedings of the SIGDIAL 2013 Conference*, pages 414–422, Metz, France, August. Association for Computational Linguistics.

Sungjin Lee. 2013. Structured Discriminative Model For Dialog State Tracking. In *Proceedings of the SIGDIAL 2013 Conference*, pages 442–451, Metz, France, August. Association for Computational Linguistics.

Andrew Ng and Michael Jordan. 2001. On discriminative vs. generative classifiers: A comparison of logistic regression and naive bayes. *Neural Information Processing Systems*, pages 841–848.

Hang Ren, Weiqun Xu, Yan Zhang, and Yonghong Yan. 2013. Dialog state tracking using conditional random fields. In *Proceedings of the SIGDIAL 2013 Conference*, pages 457–461, Metz, France, August. Association for Computational Linguistics.

Douglas L Vail, Manuela M Veloso, and John D Lafferty. 2007. Conditional Random Fields for Activity Recognition Categories and Subject Descriptors. In *Proceedings of the 6th International Joint Conference on Autonomous Agents and Multiagent systems (AAMAS 2007)*.

Zhuoran Wang and Oliver Lemon. 2013. A simple and generic belief tracking mechanism for the dialog state tracking challenge: On the believability of observed information. In *Proceedings of the SIGDIAL 2013 Conference*, pages 423–432, Metz, France, August. Association for Computational Linguistics.

Christian Wellekens. 1987. Explicit time correlation in hidden markov models for speech recognition. In *Acoustics, Speech, and Signal Processing, IEEE International Conference on ICASSP'87.*, volume 12, pages 384–386. IEEE.

Jason D Williams, Antoine Raux, Deepak Ramachandran, and Alan Black. 2012. Dialog state tracking challenge handbook.

Jason Williams, Antoine Raux, Deepak Ramachandran, and Alan Black. 2013. The Dialog State Tracking Challenge. In *Proceedings of the SIGDIAL 2013 Conference*, pages 404–413, Metz, France, August. Association for Computational Linguistics.

Jason D. Williams. 2010. Incremental partition recombination for efficient tracking of multiple dialog states. In *ICASSP*, pages 5382–5385.

Jason D. Williams. 2012a. Challenges and Opportunities for State Tracking in Statistical Spoken Dialog Systems: Results From Two Public Deployments. *IEEE Journal of Selected Topics in Signal Processing*, 6(8):959–970, December.

Jason D Williams. 2012b. A critical analysis of two statistical spoken dialog systems in public use. In *Spoken Language Technology Workshop (SLT), 2012 IEEE*, pages 55–60. IEEE.

Steve Young, Milica Gašić, Simon Keizer, François Mairesse, Jost Schatzmann, Blaise Thomson, and Kai Yu. 2010. The Hidden Information State model: A practical framework for POMDP-based spoken dialogue management. *Computer Speech & Language*, 24(2):150–174, April.

Lukáš Žilka, David Marek, Matěj Korvas, and Filip Jurčíček. 2013. Comparison of bayesian discriminative and generative models for dialogue state tracking. In *Proceedings of the SIGDIAL 2013 Conference*, pages 452–456, Metz, France, August. Association for Computational Linguistics.

Click or Type: An Analysis of Wizard's Interaction for Future Wizard Interface Design

Srinivasan Janarthanam[1], Robin Hill[2], Anna Dickinson[2], Morgan Fredriksson[3]

[1] School of Mathematical and Computer Sciences, Heriot-Watt University

[2] School of Informatics, University of Edinburgh

[3] Liquid Media AB, Stockholm

sc445@hw.ac.uk

Abstract

We present an analysis of a Pedestrian Navigation and Information dialogue corpus collected using a Wizard-of-Oz interface. We analysed how wizards preferred to communicate to users given three different options: preset buttons that can generate an utterance, sequences of buttons and dropdown lists to construct complex utterances and free text utterances. We present our findings and suggestions for future WoZ design based on our findings.

1 Introduction

Wizard-of-Oz environments (WoZ) have been become an essential tool for collecting and studying dialogue between humans pretending to be machines and human users in various domains. It is an effective way to collect dialogues between real users and dialogue systems before actually implementing the dialogue system. In this framework, participants interact with an expert human operator (known as "Wizard") who is disguised as a dialogue system. These Wizards replace one or more parts of the dialogue system such as speech recognition, natural language understanding, dialogue management, natural language generation modules and so on. Real users interact differently with humans and computers. While their expectations with human interlocutors are high and varied, they are ready to adapt and "go easy" on computers during interaction (Pearson et al., 2006). So, in a WoZ framework, the conversation between real users and the Wizards (pretending to be dialogue systems) are of an appropriate type to be used for dialogue system design and not as complex as in human-human conversation.

In order to provide a speedy response, most WoZ systems are designed in such a way that responses are hard wired to buttons so that they can be sent to the synthesizer at the touch of a button. However, in order to handle unexpected situations, most WoZ interfaces also have a free text interface that allows the Wizard to type any text to be synthesised by the synthesizer. Are free text interfaces used only under unexpected situations? In this paper, we analyse how free text interfaces are used by Wizards in a pedestrian tourist navigation and information dialogue and discuss how the results of our analysis be used to inform future WoZ designs. These dialogues were collected as a part of SpaceBook EU FP7 project.

In Section 2, we present previous work in WoZ interfaces and the domain of pedestrian navigation and information. We then present our WoZ setup and data collection in Section 3 and 4. In Section 5, we present our analysis of the corpus, issues and suggestions in Sections 6 and 7.

2 Related work

Wizard-of-Oz (WoZ) frameworks have been used since early 90s in order to collect human-computer dialogue data to help design dialogue systems (Fraser and Gilbert, 1991). WoZ systems have been used extensively to collect data to learn dialogue management policies (Rieser and Lemon, 2011) and information presentation strategies (Demberg et al., 2011).

Pedestrian navigation and information systems is a domain of interest to many mobile phone applications. Applications such as Siri, Google Maps Navigation, or Sygic deal with the task of navigation while TripAdvisor, Triposo, etc . focus on the tourist information problem. Additionally, several research prototypes have been built to generate navigation instructions (Bartie and Mackaness, 2006; Shroder et al., 2011) and to have conversations with tourists (Janarthanam et al., 2013). WoZ experiments enable the collection of realistic data to assist in the development and testing of these systems.

Figure 1: Wizard of Oz interface - Google Satellite Map and StreetView

3 WoZ setup

The wizard interface consisted a browser window showing a Google Map and Street View with the Tourists position. Google StreetView showed the Tourist's point of view (see Figure 1). The Wizard was able to communicate information to the Tourist in three different ways in the Wizard Response Panel (see Figure 2):

Hot buttons: By clicking on one of several buttons with commonly used phrases (e.g. "OK. I'll suggest a route for you", "You want to cross the road whenever you can", "Would you like further information about that?"). Buttons were organised thematically in sections such as: confirmations, ways of asking the Tourist to repeat what they had said, ways to indicate to the Tourist that the Wizard was doing something and they should wait ("Just a moment, please", "I'm just finding that out for you now" and "Apologies for the delay") and directions. The range of choices available via the buttons (there were nine different confirmations) was intended to allow the Wizard to mimic the variability of human speech; they were grouped to facilitate rapid identification and selection.

Sequences: By generating text from a sequence of drop-down menus, e.g. (where items in square brackets are drop-down lists): "You want to take the [count] [pathway] on your [direction]).

Free text: By typing free text into a text editor.

Pre-entered phrases for Hot Buttons were selected following two previous Wizard of Oz experiments where the Tourist and the Wizard communicated by voice; common expressions used during these sessions were summarised and presented on an initial evaluation interface which was evaluated with 15 dyads. Results from that experiment fed into the WoZ interface above.

At the bottom right of the screen, there was a scrollable record of the Wizard's output in case the participant needed to confirm what had been sent to the Tourist. Finally, there was a selection of system comments the Wizard could make, for example to note system problems such as problems hearing the Tourist. This information was recorded by the system but not sent to the Tourist. Additionally, screen capture software was used to record all the on-screen interaction. As a back-up, the lab was videoed on DV cassette using a tripod-mounted camcorder.

Instructions to participants were developed to encourage participants (i.e. playing the role of Tourists) to solve problems without directing them too much. e.g. "You've heard a story about a statue of a dog that you think is nearby and would like to take a photo of the dog and perhaps learn a little more about the story.", "You have arranged to have lunch with a friend in a nearby pub. You

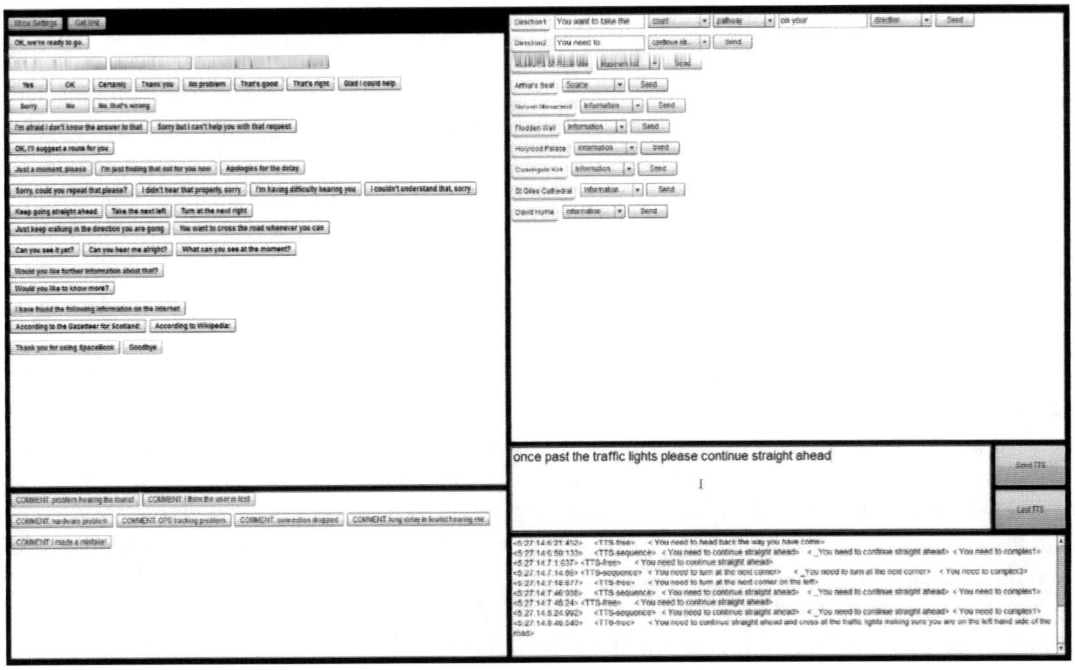

Figure 2: Wizard of Oz interface - Wizard response panel

can't remember the exact name but you are sure it had the word "Bell" in the title."

The Tourist was equipped with an Android mobile phone (Samsung Galaxy Note) and headset. The phone ran a custom-built app that sent live GPS, satellite and accelerometer data back to the WoZ system while receiving the Wizards text messages and converting them to speech. As a backup, and to ensure the reliability of the positioning data, a GPS logging application (My Tracks) also recorded the data every two seconds on the phone. Time-stamping within the files permits offline synchronisation with the speech data.

4 Data collection

Participants were enrolled using an events organising website called EventBrite[1]. Two participants attended each experimental session and were assigned to one of two roles: the Tourist or the Wizard. At the end of the experiment each received £10. Ten dyads (twenty people) completed the experiment. They were aged between 19 and 26 (mean 22), and had lived in Edinburgh between 0.7 and 10 years (mean 2.9). 8 were male, and 12 female.

After participants had arrived at the lab, they signed a consent form and provided demographic information (age, sex, and length of time in Edinburgh). The task descriptions were handed out and roles were assigned. The Wizard was given supplementary information about some of the locations and Google Map print-outs, but was instructed to make up any answers to questions asked by the Tourist if necessary.

After an initial equipment test and training, the Tourist dialled a standard Edinburgh landline number on the mobile phone which connected to a Skype account and the experiment began. If the call dropped, the Tourist would redial and continue. There was a basic set of tasks assigned to the Tourist, but they were encouraged to expand and adapt this and were free to ask any tourist or navigation-based questions that they thought of on the way.

The Tourist traversed Edinburgh on their own; the Wizard and experimenter remained in a laboratory. The Wizard used GPS information and dialogue with the Tourist to establish location. For the Wizard, the Tourist's view had to be reconstructed using the display software available. These dialogue sessions ranged between 41:56 to 66:43 minutes. The average dialogue duration (according to the transcriber) for the 10 dyads was 51min 46s.

Please note that for each run, a new pair of Wiz-

[1] www.eventbrite.com

ard and Tourist were used. Wizards were not retained to do more than one run because we wanted to collect data from a variety of human wizards in order to study variations in how each wizard dealt with the navigation task.

5 Corpus analysis

We analysed the corpus collected based on the three types of response generation mechanisms: hot buttons, sequences and free text, to understand their relative utility. We wanted to explore whether pre-configured text was used when available, or whether the user's interaction with the pre-configured and free text sections of the interface were influenced by other considerations than availability.

Analysis showed that buttons corresponding to preset utterances were used only 33% (+/- 14) of the time. Although wizards had the option of constructing complex utterances using a sequence of drop down lists, they only used such sequences 9% (+/- 9) of the time. 58% (+/-19) of Wizard utterances were generated using the free text interface. This may imply that the buttons did not offer what the Wizards wanted to say; in which case, we would anticipate that their self-created utterances would be very different from those pre-configured.

Individual differences: Use of the button interface varied between Wizards, with some using it very rarely and others depending on it when it provided a feature they required. The highest was 82.7% while the lowest use of free text was 31.7%. Table 1 shows that 6 out of 10 Wizards used the free text interface more than 60% of the time. It is likely that these differences were due to individual variations such as speed of typing and comfort with using an array of buttons.

Usage of free text interface	Wizard count
Below 30%	0
30-40%	3
40-50%	1
50-60%	0
60-70%	3
70-80%	1
80-90%	2

Table 1: Usage of free text interface

As an example of these individual differences, one Wizard used the button-press interface only once during the first navigation task (to ask "What can you see at the moment?"), choosing to direct the Tourist almost exclusively through use of the free text interface. By contrast, of the twelve Wizard utterances in another session's initial navigation task, only two were free text. It is interesting to note, however, that the Tourist commented "I've a feeling (the Wizard) is laughing at me right now."

5.1 Hot button interface

We analysed how frequently each hot button in the interface was used by Wizards. We also counted how frequently the same text as the buttons was generated using the free text interface. This will show us if Wizards tend to type the same text that can effectively be generated at the push of a hot button. The following table shows the frequency of each hot button used over the 10 dialogues that we analysed.

There were forty buttons in total. Two initial buttons intended to be used at the start of the experiment or when the call was restarted after a problem: "Okay, we are ready to go. Please pretend to have just dialed Space Book and say hello." and "Hello, SpaceBook speaking." (These were used 29 times) and two intended for the end of the call: "Thank you for using SpaceBook" and "Goodbye" (10 times). Table 2 shows the frequency of usage for other hot buttons.

Utterance type	Frequency
Confirmation (e.g. Yes, Okay, Certainly)	168
Navigation (e.g. "Keep going straight ahead")	114
Filler (e.g. "Just a moment please")	60
Repeat request (e.g. "Sorry, could you repeat that please?")	34
Visual checks ("Can you see it yet?"/ "What can you see at the moment?")	32
Offer of further information/ help	30
References (e.g. "According to Wikipedia")	20
Negation ("No", "No, that's wrong")	18
Failure ("I'm afraid I don't know the answer to that")	8

Table 2: Usage of Hot Buttons

The above table presents a Zipfian curve with some utterances such as "Okay", "Keep going straight ahead" having high frequency and some utterances such as "I'm afraid I don't know the answer to that," "I couldn't understand that, sorry" with extremely low frequency. Even the highest frequency utterance, "Okay" was only used about 5 times per session on average. This does not mean that the Wizard acknowledged the subject at such low frequency but, as the analysis below indicates, decided to acknowledge the user with free text-generated utterances.

5.2 Free text utterances

We analysed the free text utterances generated by the Wizards. This analysis, we believe, could show us how to build better Wizard interfaces for collecting dialogue data for pedestrian navigation. First, we counted the number of free text utterances that duplicated Hot Button text. Then, we analysed the other utterances generated using the free text interface.

Table 3 presents the frequency of utterances that were generated using the free text interface but were the same as hot button text. The table shows that even though there are hot buttons for utterances such as "Yes", "Sorry", Wizards tended to type them into the free text interface. In some cases these words were followed by a more complex utterance which the Wizard had chosen to deliver as a single statement (e.g. "Yes, that's the way to go.", "no, you should turn around"), and second, these utterances are short and could easily be typed rather than searching for the corresponding hot button. Also, Wizards sometimes used alternative spellings for words such as "Okay" which could be produced using a hot button. The word "Ok" was used 15 times in 10 sessions.

Text	Frequency
Yes	45
Sorry	21
No	21
Take the next left	4
No problem	3
Certainly	2
Thank you	1

Table 3: Usage of Free Text for utterances same as Hot Buttons

In addition, Wizards use free text to generate utterances that are paraphrases of hot button utterances, such as:

- "Keep going", "Just keep walking", etc
- "Great", "Excellent", etc
- "One moment", "Wait a second please", etc
- "Of course"
- "Okay cool"

These analyses imply that free text is not accessed only in the last resort because the user cannot find the hot button that says what they'd like to say. Clearly, the interaction is more complex and concerns both speed (the contrast of typing a short utterance such as "Yes" compared with the time needed to discover the correct button on a display and navigate to it with a mouse) and the user's imposition of their own identity on the conversation; where the hot button interface offered several confirmatory utterances, users often used their own (e.g. "Great, "Excellent", "Cool"), utterances which were, presumably, part of the way these Wizards more normally interacted with peers.

In this section, we present the other types of utterances Wizards generated using the free text interface.

1) Check user's location:
Wizards asked several free text questions to check where the user was, given that the positioning system on smartphones was not entirely accurate. They framed most questions as yes/no check questions and enriched them with situational cues (e.g."Is the Pear Tree on your right?", "Have you reached the Royal Mile yet?", "Can you see Nicolson Square?", "Have you passed the primary school on your left?").

2) Informing user's location:
Wizards sometimes informed users of their location. e.g. "This is West Nicolson Street".

3) Complex navigation instructions:
Using the free text interface, Wizards generated a variety of complex navigation instructions that were not covered by the hot buttons. These include instructions where the subject was asked to carry out two instructions in sequence (e.g. "Turn left, and keep walking until you get to Chapel Street"), orienting the user (e.g. "You want the road on your right", "Please go back in the direction you came from"), signaling to the user that he/she was walking in the wrong direction (e.g. "You're going the wrong way"), a priori instructions to destination (e.g. "To get there you will need to keep going up the Royal Mile. Then turn left at the junction between North and South Bridge. Walk up South Bridge, and it will change to Nicolson Street. Surgeon's Hall will be on the left hand side.").

Some navigation instructions were complex because they were not general instructions but direct responses to the Tourist's question. One example of this was by Dynamic Earth (dyad 07) when the Wizard told the Tourist to follow a footpath. Tourist: "One of the footpaths banks to the right, and the other goes straight forward. Which one?", the Wizard answered: "You want the one that is straight forward."

The navigation directions on hot buttons were necessarily very general (e.g. Keep going straight ahead/ Take the next left) and Wizards frequently used the free text to enrich the directions and make them more specific, e.g. (dyad 09) "Walk down Crichton Street towards the Mosque." In the initial navigation task, this Wizard used the free text interface 7 times, and the navigation hot buttons only 4 times. Each segment of free text enriched the interaction by providing specific navigational information, so where the Wizard could have selected the hot button for "Keep going straight", instead she chose to add value to the interaction through the use of place names and typed, "Continue straight onto West Richmond Street".

A similar pattern can be seen in the interaction in dyad 10 where the Wizard used the free text option to navigate the Tourist according to objects in his environment. e.g. "Turn right at the traffic lights" and "Walk straight down past the Bingo on your left.". Of the 22 Wizard utterances in the first navigation task in the dyad, only 5 were hot buttons. 14 were navigation instructions, of which 3 were button-presses and one ("Walk straight on") paraphrased an existing button. The Tourist got lost in this task, so there was also some checking on his location.

These are not isolated examples. In total, over the ten dyads, 308 utterances from the total 927 free text utterances were Wizards "enriching" their navigation directions by adding contextual cues, most commonly the name of the street or a landmark to help situate the Tourist. For example, "You can reach it by turning right down Holyrood Road at the junction.", "Please head towards the Mosque".

Although 33% of overall free text utterances were enriched navigation instructions, this overall pattern varied depending on the dyad, ranging from dyad 03 where 62.5% were enriched instructions, to dyad 08, where only 8% were enriched.

These value-added uses of the free text suggest that the addition of contextual cues is regarded as important by the individuals acting as Wizards. An improved WoZ interface might seek to support such utterances.

4) Reassuring user:
Wizards presented information such as landmarks users can see as they walk along to reassure them that they are on the right track (e.g. "You will pass Richmond Place on your left", "You will walk past the Canongate Kirk on your right beforehand").

5) Informing time/distance to destination:
Wizards presented how long it will take to reach the destination to set the right expectation in the user's mind (e.g. "It will be about a two minute walk", "the gym is 200 metres along this road on your right").

6) Providing destination information:
Wizards provided information about the location of destination in reference to the user (e.g. "And Bonsai Bar Bistro will be on the left, just before you reach The Pleasance", "The Museum of Edinburgh will be on the left") or other landmarks (e.g. "The Scottish Parliament is next to Our Dynamic Earth", "The entrance is on the other side"). Note that this interaction, too, is normally enriched by situational cues.

7) Informing destinations that match search criteria:
Some tasks presented to subjects did not specify the actual name of the destination. Hence when they asked the Wizard for a matching destination, Wizards used free text to suggest destinations that match the search criteria (e.g. "There is a restaurant called Bonsai Bistro", "There are three museums to visit. They are Museum of Edinburgh, People's Story Museum, and Museum of Childhood").

8) Check if destination reached and identified:
Wizards checked whether users had reached their destination by asking them to confirm if they had (e.g. "Have you reached it?", "Have you found the sports centre?"). The hot button "Can you see it yet?" covered this functionality, but once more, free text allowed the user to increase situational specificity by identifying the target.

9) Additional information about landmarks:
Wizards presented additional information about landmarks such as its name ("the hill besides par-

liament is in fact 2 hills, the rocky cliffs you can see are called crags", "behind that is arthurs seat"), the year it was built/opened (e.g. "it was opened in 1999"), what it functions as (e.g. "offices for a newspaper publisher").

In some cases such free text utterances were produced in response to questions asked by Tourists. For example, when the Tourist of dyad 05 passed the Fringe office, they asked, "Do you know what dates the Fringe is on this year?". The Wizard used free text to answer the question. Later in the same experiment, the Tourist identified Vodka Rev as a landmark ("Down past Vodka Rev?") and the Wizard responded with free text about the landmark: "Vodka Rev does half price food on Mondays.".

10) Signalling connection problems:
Wizards informed users when they lost the user's GPS signal (e.g. "hold on 1 second, gps connection gone") and to establish contact and check user's attention (e.g. "hello?", "I can't hear you at the moment").

Further, some Wizards used the free text to humanise the person-to-person element of the interaction. They would chat to Tourists, make jokes ("I cannot answer rhetorical questions, as I am both a computer and aware they are not meant to be answered.") and in one case, invite the Tourist out for a drink.

6 Issues with free text

As one can imagine, there are issues with free text utterances generated by Wizards.

Spelling:
Several words used in free text utterances were misspelled. e.g. "roundabaout", "entrace", "plesae", "toewards", "You want ot cross the roD") etc. These ranged from 0 to 13 errors per session with a mean of 3.6 (+/- 3.9) errors per session. Adjacent words were sometimes joined together (e.g. "atyour", "upahead", etc) and sometimes incorrectly segmented with space (e.g. "collection sof", "hea ryou", etc). Some entity names were misspelled as well (e.g. "Critchon", "Dyanmic Earth", "artthurs seat", etc). Spelling errors can reflect poorly when the utterances are synthesized and the misspelled words mispronounced.

Syntax:
We also found a few syntactic errors in utterance construction (e.g. "Continue going Chambers street"). Similar to spelling errors, utterances with improper syntax can sound weird to the Tourist and could lead to confusion and misunderstanding instructions.

Incorrect entity names:
Wizards did not always get street names correct, e.g. in dyad 02, the Wizard directed the Tourist to "Nicholas Square" and the Tourist needed to seek clarification that he meant "Nicolson Square".

Time and effort:
It takes time and can slow the interaction with the user, leading to issues like interruptions and the flow of the conversation being upset.

7 Suggestions

Based on the above analysis, we propose a list of suggestions to build a better Wizard of Oz interface for collecting dialogues concerning pedestrian navigation and exploration. The objective of the WoZ system is to provide an effective interface to Wizards to interact with Tourists while pretending to be dialogue systems. One of the important requirements is that Wizards should be able to generate context appropriate utterances quickly to make the dialogue appear more natural without unnecessary lag between a user's requests and the system's responses. Hot buttons are designed so that the utterance can generated at the push of a button. However as our data shows, Wizards tended to use the free text interface about 60% of the time.

While there are situations in which free text is necessary, in general it risks slowing the interaction and potentially confusing the Tourist when words are mis-spelled or omitted. In addition, supporting the Wizard more effectively with an improved WoZ interface is likely to permit them to spend more time supporting and informing the Tourist. Free text utterances can lead to slow system response and there is therefore a need to find a compromise between the two. We have the following suggestions:

1. More hot buttons:
Some utterances generated using the free text interface could not be generated using the hot but-

tons or the sequences. These include reassuring users, informing them of the time/distance to destination, informing them of search results, etc. While free text is a useful interface to Wizards to generate unforeseen utterances, more hot buttons covering new functionality can be faster to use.

However, introducing additional hot buttons would add complexity to the interface, which is likely to have the undesireable effect of encouraging users to avoid the cluttered display in favour if the straightforward free text interface. One partial solution is to ensure that buttons are organised and grouped in ways that are intuitive for the Wizard. This, and the optimum number of buttons for the display, should be investigated experimentally.

2. Multi functional hot buttons:
Some free text utterances were complex versions of simple utterances that were already covered by hot buttons. For instance, utterances like "Keep going up Nicolson Street" or "Keep walking until you get to Chapel Street" can be seen as a version of "Keep going straight ahead" but with some appended information (i.e. street name, landmark).

The interface could be designed so that hot button utterances could be modified or appended with more information. For example, a single click the hot button might send the utterance to the free text editor, allowing the Wizard to add more information, whereas a double click would send the utterance directly to the TTS.

3. Spell check, grammar check and auto correction:
To ensure that the speech synthesizer works as effectively as possible, the utterances typed in the free text editor must be correctly spelled. One solution to the frequent mis-spelling made by Wizards typing at speed is to automatically spell check and correct text typed in the free text interface.

Ensuring that text is correct would reduce the risk of the speech synthesizer mispronouncing misspelt names and words. Similarly, a grammar check would mean that the synthesised utterances felt more natural.

Since there is the danger of an automatic spell checker making mistakes, the spell check and correction should happen when the Wizard finishes typing a word or utterance and the auto corrected word or utterance be shown to the Wizard before it is sent to the TTS.

4. Autocomplete:
Autocomplete is a feature that predicts the next words the user intends to type based on those already typed. It is currently used by search engines such as Google to complete users' search queries based on their search history and profile. A similar feature that can complete utterances taking into account the user's request, dialogue history, and the spatial context could speed up the response time of the Wizard.

5. Location aware WoZ interface:
The WoZ system could be "aware" of the user's surroundings. Such a solution might enable the interface to have dynamically changing buttons, so when the user is headed up Nicolson Street, the "Keeping going" button could have Nicolson Street on it. Information about entities around the user can also be assigned to hot buttons dynamically. However, hot buttons with dynamically changing labels and functionality could be cognitively overloading to Wizards.

Of course, the addition of such functionality to the WoZ interface must be carefully evaluated. A dynamic interface may be harder to learn, and increasing the number of buttons may, counter-intuitively, mean that users are less likely to select hot buttons because the effort to scan the array of buttons is greater than the effort needed to type utterances, particularly short ones, into a free text box.

8 Conclusion

In this paper, we presented a Wizard of Oz system that was used to collect dialogues in the domain of pedestrian navigation and information. We analysed the corpus collected to identify how Wizards preferred to interact with the pedestrian users and why. We identified issues with free text interfaces that was used by majority of Wizards and suggested improvements towards future Wizard interface design.

Acknowledgments

The research leading to these results was funded by the European Commission's Framework 7 programme under grant agreement no. 270019 (SPACEBOOK project).

References

P. Bartie and W. Mackaness. 2006. Development of a speech-based augmented reality system to support exploration of cityscape. *Transactions in GIS*, 10:63–86.

Vera Demberg, Andi Winterboer, and Johanna D. Moore. 2011. A strategy for information presentation in spoken dialog systems. *Comput. Linguist.*, 37(3):489–539, September.

N. Fraser and G. N. Gilbert. 1991. Simulating speech systems. *Computer Speech and Language*, 5:81–99.

S. Janarthanam, O. Lemon, P. Bartie, T. Dalmas, A. Dickinson, X. Liu, W. Mackaness, and B. Webber. 2013. Evaluating a city exploration dialogue system combining question-answering and pedestrian navigation. In *Proc. ACL 2013*.

J. Pearson, J. Hu, H. P. Branigan, M. J. Pickering, and C. Nass. 2006. Adaptive language behavior in HCI: how expectations and beliefs about a system affect users' word choice. In *Proceedings of the SIGCHI conference on Human Factors in computing systems, Montral.*

V. Rieser and O. Lemon. 2011. Learning and Evaluation of Dialogue Strategies for new Applications: Empirical Methods for Optimization from Small Data Sets. *Computational Linguistics*, 37:1.

C.J. Shroder, W. Mackaness, and B. Gittings. 2011. Giving the Right Route Directions: The Requirements for Pedestrian Navigation Systems. *Transactions in GIS*, pages 419–438.

Recipes for building voice search UIs for automotive

Martin Labsky, Ladislav Kunc, Tomas Macek, Jan Kleindienst, Jan Vystrcil
IBM Prague Research and Development Lab
V Parku 2294/4, 148 00 Prague 4
Czech Republic
{martin.labsky, ladislav_kunc1, tomas_macek, jankle, jan_vystrcil}@cz.ibm.com

Abstract

In this paper we describe a set of techniques we found suitable for building multi-modal search applications for automotive environments. As these applications often search across different topical domains, such as maps, weather or Wikipedia, we discuss the problem of switching focus between different domains. Also, we propose techniques useful for minimizing the response time of the search system in mobile environment. We evaluate some of the proposed techniques by means of usability tests with 10 novice test subjects who drove a simulated lane change test on a driving simulator. We report results describing the induced driving distraction and user acceptance.

1 Introduction

The task of designing mobile search user interfaces (UIs) that combine multiple application domains (such as navigation, POI and web search) is significantly harder than just placing all single domain solutions adjacent to one another. We propose and evaluate a set of UI techniques useful for implementing such systems. The techniques are exemplified using a prototype multimodal search assistant tailored for in-car use. The prototype supports several application domains including navigation and POI search, Wikipedia, weather forecasts and car owner's manual. Finally, we report usability evaluation results using this prototype.

2 Related Work

Two examples of multi-modal search UIs for automotive are the Toyota Entune[1] and the Honda Link[2]. Both infotainment systems integrate a set of dedicated mobile applications including a browser, navigation, music services, stocks, weather or traffic information. Both use a tablet or a smartphone to run the mobile applications which brings the advantage of faster upgrades of the in-car infotainment suite. Home screens of these systems consist of a matrix of square tiles that correspond to individual applications.

The answers presented to the user should only contain highly relevant information, e.g. presenting only points of interest that are near the current location. This is called conversational maxim of relevance (Paul, 1975). Many other lessons learned by evaluating in-car infotainment systems are discussed in (Green, 2013).

In recent years, personal assistant systems like Siri (Aron, 2011), Google Now! (Google, 2013) and the Dragon Mobile Assistant (Nuance, 2013) started to penetrate the automotive environment. Most of these applications are being enhanced with driving modes to enable safer usage while driving. Dragon Mobile Assistant can detect whether the user is in a moving car and automatically switches to "Driver Mode" that relies on speech recognition and text-to-speech feedback. Siri recently added spoken presentation of incoming text messages and voice mail, and it also allows to dictate responses. Besides the speech-activated assistant functionality, Google Now! tries to exploit various context variables (e.g. location history, user's calendar, search history). Context is used for pro-active reminders that pop-up in the right time and place. Speech recognition of Google Now! has an interesting feature that tries to act upon incomplete/interim recognition results; sometimes the first answer is however not the right one which is later detected and the answer is replaced when results are refined.

[1] http://www.toyota.com/entune/

[2] http://owners.honda.com/hondalink/nextgeneration

3 UI techniques to support search while driving

Below we present selected techniques we found useful while designing and testing prototype search UIs for automotive.

3.1 Nearly stateless VUI

While driving and interacting with an application UI, it often happens that the driver must interrupt interaction with the system due to a sudden increase of cognitive load associated with the primary task of driving. The interaction is either postponed or even abandoned. The UI activity may later be resumed but often the driver will not remember the context where s/he left off. In heavily state-based systems such as those based on hierarchical menus, reconstruction of application context in the driver's mind may be costly and associated with multiple glances at the display.

In order to minimize the need for memorizing or reconstructing the application context, we advocate UIs that are as stateless as possible from the user's point of view. In the context of spoken input, this means the UI should be able to process all voice input regardless of its state.

This is important so that the driver does not need to recall the application state before s/he utters a request. For instance, being able to ask "Where can we get a pizza" only after changing screen to "POI search" can be problematic as the driver (1) needs to change screens, (2) needs to remember what the current screen is, and (3) may need to look at the display to check the screen state. All of these issues may increase driver distraction (its haptic, visual and mental components).

3.2 Self-sufficient auditory channel

According to the subjective results of usability tests described in Section 6 and according to earlier work on automotive dictation (Macek et al., 2013), many drivers were observed to rely primarily on the audio-out channel to convey information from the UI while driving and they also preferred it to looking at a display. A similar observation was made also for test drivers who listened to and navigated news articles and short stories (Kunc et al., 2014).

Two recommendations could be abstracted from the above user tests. First, the UI should produce verbose audio output that fully describes what happens with the system (in cases when the driver controls the UI while driving). This includes spoken output as well as earcons indicating important micro-states of the system such as "listening" or "processing". Second, the UI should enable the user to easily replay what has been said by the system, e.g. by pressing a button, to offset the serial character of spoken output. These steps should make it possible for selected applications to run in a display-less mode while driving or at least minimize the number of gazes at the display.

3.3 Distinguish domain transition types

By observing users accessing functions of multiple applications through a common UI, we observed several characteristic transition types.

Hierarchical. The user navigates a menu tree, often guided by GUI hints.

Within domain. Users often perform multiple interactions within one application, such as performing several Wikipedia queries, refining them and browsing the retrieved results.

Application switching. Aware of the namings of the applications supported by the system, users often switch explicitly to a chosen domain before uttering a domain-specific command.

Direct task invocation. Especially in case of UIs having a unifying persona like Siri (Aron, 2011), users do not view the system as a set of applications and instead directly request app-specific functions, regardless of their past interaction.

Subdialog. The user requests functionality out of the current application domain. The corresponding application is invoked to handle the request and then the focus returns automatically to the original domain. Examples include taking a note or checking the weather forecast while in the middle of another task.

Undo. A combined "undo" or "go back" feature accessible globally at a key press proved useful during our usability testing to negate any unwanted actions accidentally triggered.

Figure 1 shows samples for the above transition types using an example multi-domain search assistant further described in Section 4. Similar lists of transition types ware described previously, e.g. (Milward et al., 2006). Based on observing human interactions with our prototype system, we built a simple probabilistic model to control the likelihood of the system taking each of the above transition types, and used it to rescore the results of the ASR and NLU systems.

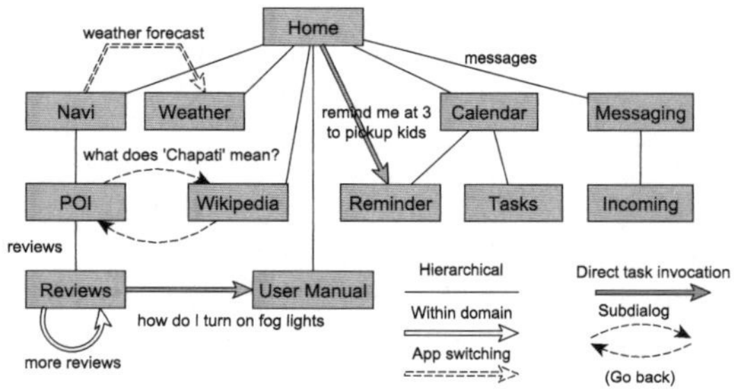

Figure 1: Transitions in a multi-domain system.

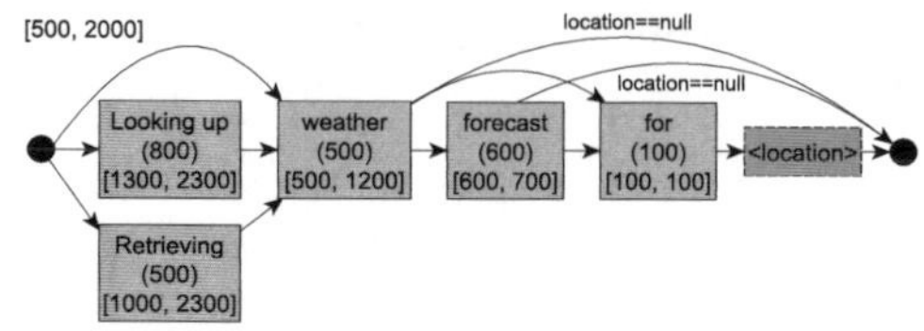

Figure 2: Sample incremental prompt graph. Segments are annotated with durations in round brackets and min/max times before an unknown slot value has to be spoken (ms).

3.4 Early and incremental feedback about the application state

Mobile search UIs often depend both on local and remote resources such as ASR and NLU services and various data providers. In mobile environments, availability and response times of remote services may vary significantly. Most mobile UIs address this problem by responding with a beep and displaying a "processing" sign until the final answer is rendered. We describe a UI technique that combines redundant local and remote resources (ASR and NLU) to quickly come up with a partial meaningful response that addresses the user's request. Chances are that the first response based on partial understanding is wrong and the following prompt must correct it.

Figure 2 shows a template definition for a system prompt that starts playing once the system is confident enough about the user's intent being a weather forecast question. The system provides forecasts for the current location by default but can switch to other locations if specified by the user. Supposing the system is equipped with real-time ASR and NLU that quickly determine the high-level intent of the user, such as "weather forecast", the initial part of the prompt can start playing almost immediately after the user has stopped speaking. While a prefix of this prompt is playing, more advanced ASR and NLU models deliver a finer-grained and more precise interpretation of the input, including any slot-value pairs like "location=London". Once this final interpretation is known, the playback can be directed via the shortest path to the identified variable prompt segments like `<location>`. Further, the selection of prompt prefix to be played can be guided by a current estimate of service delays to minimize chances of potential pauses before speaking prompt segments whose values are not yet known.

4 Voice search assistant prototype

In this section we briefly present a voice search interface that was developed by incrementaly implementing the four UI techniques presented above. While interim versions of this system were only evaluated subjectively, formal evaluation results are presented for the final version in Section 6.

The voice search assistant covers six application domains shown in Figure 3. Navigation services include spoken route guidance together with unified destination entry by voice (addresses and POIs). Some POIs are accompanied by user reviews that can be read out as part of POI details.

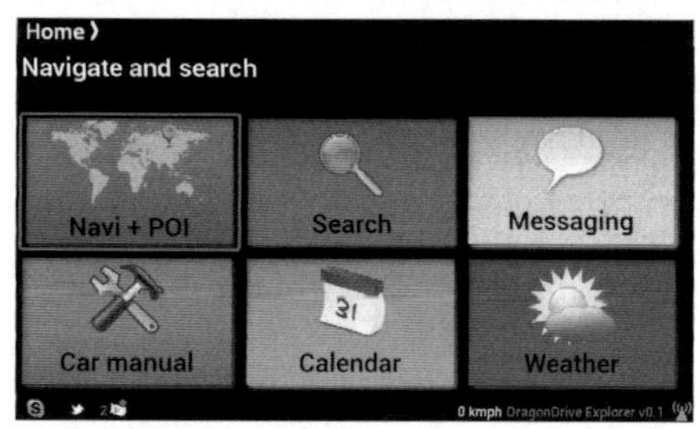

Figure 3: Prototype home screen (apps as tiles).

Further, the user can search various knowledge sources like Wikipedia, Wolfram Alpha and the web. The retrieved results are pre-processed and the first one is played back to the user with the possibility of navigating the result list.

To simulate asynchronous events, the system reads out Skype text messages. The driver can also create location and time based reminders that pop up during the journey.

Finally, the system supports full-text search over the car owner's manual. Relevant text passages are read out and displayed based on a problem description or question uttered by the driver.

5 Usability testing setup and procedure

A low-fidelity driving simulator setup similar to the one described in (Curin et al., 2011) was used to conduct lane change tests using (Mattes, 2003). Tests were conducted with 10 novice subjects and took approximately 1 hour and 20 minutes per participant. At the beginning and at the end of the test, subjects filled in pre-test and post-test questionnaires. Before the actual test, each participant practised both driving and using the prototype for up to 20 minutes. The evaluated test consisted of four tasks: an initial undistracted drive (used to adapt a custom LCT ideal path for each participant), two distracted driving trips in counter-balanced order, and a final undistracted drive (used for evaluation). Each of the four drives was performed at constant speed of 60km/h and took about 3.5 minutes. During the distracted driving tasks, the users were instructed verbally to perform several search tasks using the prototype. During task 1, subjects had to set destination to "office", then find a pharmacy along the route, check the weather forecast and take a note about the forecast conditions. Task 2 only differed slightly by having a different destination and POI, and by the user searching Wikipedia instead of asking about weather.

6 Usability testing results

Objective distraction was measured using mean deviation ($MDev$) and standard deviation ($SDLP$) of the vehicle's lateral position (Mattes, 2003). Two versions of both statistics were obtained: overall (computed over the whole trip) and using lane-keeping segments only. The graph in Figure 4 shows averaged results for the final undistracted drive and for the first and second distracted driving tasks (reflecting the order of the tasks, not their types). We observe that using the search UI led to significant distraction during lane change segments but not during lane keeping. Also, the distraction results for the first trip show higher variance which we attribute to the users still adapting to the driving simulator and to using the UI. The observed distraction levels are comparable to our earlier results obtained for a text dictation UI when used with a GUI display (Curin et al., 2011).

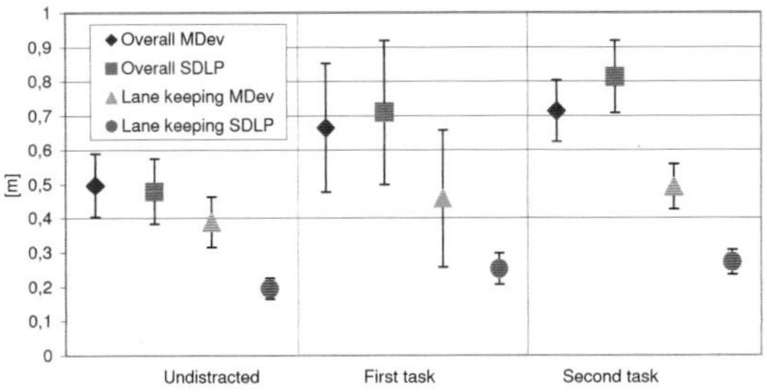

Figure 4: Driving distraction while using a multimodal search UI.

Several observations came out of the subjective feedback collected using forms. The users reported extensive use of the auditory channel (both in and out) only with occasional glimpses at the screen (we however observed that objectively they looked at the display more often than they reported subjectively). Users also missed some information in the voice output channel such as audio indication of route calculation progress (which could take several seconds). Reading any text from the screen was found difficult, and users requested that playback be improved; see related follow-up study (Kunc et al., 2014). Interestingly, multiple participants requested voice commands that would duplicate buttons like "next" and "previous", even in cases where speech would be less efficient. This may show a tendency to stick with a single modality as described by (Suhm et al., 2001). Additionally, the users requested better synchronization of navigation announcements like "take exit 4 in 200 metres" with the output of other applications. The baseline behaviour utilized in the test was that high-priority navigation prompts interrupted the output of other applications. Navigation, POI search, simple note-taking and constrained search domains like weather and Wikipedia were found most useful (in this order). Open web search and browsing an original car owner's manual were considered too distracting to use while driving.

7 Conclusion

We described several recipes for building spoken search applications for automotive and exemplified them on a prototype search UI. Early usability testing results for the prototype were presented. Our future work focuses on improving the introduced techniques and exploring alternative UI paradigms (Macek et al., 2013).

Acknowledgement

The presented work is part of an IBM and Nuance joint research project.

References

Jacob Aron. 2011. How innovative is apple's new voice assistant, siri? *New Scientist*, 212(2836):24.

J. Curin, M. Labsky, T. Macek, J. Kleindienst, H. Young, A. Thyme-Gobbel, H. Quast, and L. Koenig. 2011. Dictating and editing short texts while driving: distraction and task completion. In *Proceedings of the 3rd International Conference on Automotive User Interfaces and Interactive Vehicular Applications*.

Google. 2013. Google now assistant. Available at `http://www.google.com/landing/now/`.

Paul A Green. 2013. Development and evaluation of automotive speech interfaces: useful information from the human factors and the related literature. *International Journal of Vehicular Technology*, 2013.

L. Kunc, M. Labsky, T. Macek, J. Vystrcil, J. Kleindienst, T. Kasparova, D. Luksch, and Z. Medenica. 2014. Long text reading in a car. In *Proceedings of the 16th International Conference on Human-Computer Interaction Conference (HCII)*.

Tomáš Macek, Tereza Kašparová, Jan Kleindienst, Ladislav Kunc, Martin Labský, and Jan Vystrčil. 2013. Mostly passive information delivery in a car. In *Proceedings of the 5th International Conference on Automotive User Interfaces and Interactive Vehicular Applications*, AutomotiveUI '13, pages 250–253, New York, NY, USA. ACM.

Stefan Mattes. 2003. The lane-change-task as a tool for driver distraction evaluation. In *Proceedings of the Annual Spring Conference of the GFA/ISOES*, volume 2003.

David Milward, Gabriel Amores, Nate Blaylock, Staffan Larsson, Peter Ljunglof, Pilar Manchon, and Guillermo Perez. 2006. D2.2: Dynamic multimodal interface reconfiguration. In *Talk and Look: Tools for Ambient Linguistic Knowledge IST-507802 Deliverable D2.2*.

Nuance. 2013. Dragon mobile assistant. Available at `http://www.dragonmobileapps.com`.

Grice H Paul. 1975. Logic and conversation. *Syntax and semantics*, 3:41–58.

Bernhard Suhm, Brad Myers, and Alex Waibel. 2001. Multimodal error correction for speech user interfaces. *ACM Transactions on Computer-Human Interaction (TOCHI)*, 8(1):60–98.

A Natural Language Instructor for pedestrian navigation based in generation by selection

Santiago Avalos
LIIS Group, FaMAF
Universidad Nacional de Córdoba
Córdoba, Argentina
santiagoe.avalos@gmail.com

Luciana Benotti
LIIS Group, FaMAF
Universidad Nacional de Córdoba
Córdoba, Argentina
luciana.benotti@gmail.com

Abstract

In this paper we describe a method for developing a virtual instructor for pedestrian navigation based on real interactions between a human instructor and a human pedestrian. A virtual instructor is an agent capable of fulfilling the role of a human instructor, and its goal is to assist a pedestrian in the accomplishment of different tasks within the context of a real city. The instructor decides what to say using a generation by selection algorithm, based on a corpus of real interactions generated within the world of interest. The instructor is able to react to different requests by the pedestrian. It is also aware of the pedestrian position with a certain degree of uncertainty, and it can use different city landmarks to guide him.

1 Introduction and previous work

Virtual instructors are conversational agents that help a user perform a task. These agents can be useful for many purposes, such as language learning (Nunan, 2004), training in simulated environments (Kim et al., 2009) and entertainment (Dignum, 2012; Jan et al., 2009).

Navigation agents generate verbal route directions for users to go from point A to point B in a given world. The wide variety of techniques to accomplish this task, range from giving complete route directions (all route information in a single instruction), to full interactive dialogue systems which give incremental instructions based on the position of the pedestrian. Although it can recognize pre-established written requests, the instructor presented in this work is not able to interpret utterances from the pedestrian, leaving it unable to generate a full dialogue. The instructor's decisions are based on the pedestrian actual task, his position in the world, and the previous behavior from different human instructors. In order to guide a user while performing a task, an effective instructor must know how to describe what needs to be done in a way that accounts for the nuances of the virtual world and that is enough to engage the trainee or gamer in the activity.

There are two main approaches toward automatically producing instructions. One is the selection approach, in which the task is to pick the appropriate output from a corpus of possible outputs. The other is the composition approach, in which the output is dynamically assembled using some composition procedure, e.g. grammar rules.

The natural language generation algorithm used in this work is a modified version of the generation by selection method described in (Benotti and Denis, 2011).

The advantages of generation by selection are many: it affords the use of complex and human-like sentences, the system is not bound to use written instructions (it may easily use recorded audio clips, for example), and finally, no rule writing by a dialogue expert or manual annotations is needed. The disadvantage of generation by selection is that the resulting dialogue may not be fully coherent (Shawar and Atwell, 2003; Shawar and Atwell, 2005; Gandhe and Traum, 2007).

In previous work, the selection approach to generation has been used in non task-oriented conversational agents such as negotiating agents (Gandhe and Traum, 2007), question answering characters (Leuski et al., 2006) and virtual patients (Kenny et al., 2007). In the work presented in this paper, the conversational agent is task-oriented.

In Section 2 we introduce the framework used in the interaction between the navigation agent and the human pedestrians. We discuss the creation of the human interaction corpus and the method for natural language generation in Section 3; And in Section 4 we explain the evaluation methods and the expected results.

2 The GRUVE framework

One of the major problems in developing systems that generate navigation instructions for pedestrians is evaluating them with real users in the real world. This evaluations are expensive, time consuming, and need to be carried out not just at the end of the project but also during the development cycle.

Consequently, there is a need for a common platform to effectively compare the performances of several verbal navigation systems developed by different teams using a variety of techniques.

The GIVE challenge developed a 3D virtual indoor environment for development and evaluation of indoor pedestrian navigation instruction systems (Byron et al., 2007; Koller et al., 2007). In this framework, users walk through a building with rooms and corridors, and interact with the world by pressing buttons. The user is guided by a navigation system that generates route instructions.

The GRUVE framework presented in (Janarthanam et al., 2012) is a web-based environment containing a simulated real world in which users can simulate walking on the streets of real cities whilst interacting with different navigation systems. This system focus on providing a simulated environment where people can look at landmarks and navigate based on spatial and visual instructions provided to them. GRUVE also provides a embedded navigation agent, the Buddy System, which can be used to test the framework. Apart from the virtual environment in which they are based an important difference between GIVE and GRUVE is that, in GRUVE, there is a certain degree of uncertainty about the position of the user.

Figure 1: Snapshot of the GRUVE web-client.

GRUVE presents navigation tasks in a game-world overlaid on top of the simulated real world. The main task consists of a treasure hunting similar to the one presented in GIVE. In our work, we use a modified version of the original framework, in which the main task has been replaced by a set of navigation tasks.

The web-client (see Figure 1) includes an interaction panel that lets the user interact with his navigation system. In addition to user location information, users can also interact with the navigation system using a fixed set or written utterances. The interaction panel provided to the user consists of a GUI panel with buttons and drop-lists which can be used to construct and send requests to the system in form of abstract semantic representations (dialogue actions).

3 The virtual instructor

The virtual instructor is a natural language agent that must help users reach a desired destination within the virtual world. Our method for developing an instructor consists of two phases: an annotation phase and a selection phase. In Section 3.1 we describe the annotation phase. This is performed only once, when the instructor is created, and it consists of automatically generating a corpus formed by associations between each instruction and the reaction to it. In Section 3.2 we describe how the utterance selection is performed every time the virtual instructor generates an instruction.

3.1 Annotation

As described in (Benotti and Denis, 2011), the corpus consists in recorded interactions between two people in two different roles: the Direction Giver (DG), who has knowledge of how to perform the task, and creates the instructions, and the Direction Follower (DF), who travels through the environment following those instructions.

The representation of the virtual world is given by a graph of nodes, each one representing an intersection between two streets in the city. GRUVE provides a planner that can calculate the optimal path from any starting point to a selected destination (this plan consists in the list of nodes the user must travel to reach the desired destination). As the DF user walks through the environment, he cannot change the world that surrounds him. This simplifies the automatic annotation process, and the logged atoms are:

- user position: latitude and longitude, indicating position relative to the world.
- user orientation: angle between 0-360, indicating rotation of the point of view.

In order to define the reaction associated to each utterance, it is enough to consider the position to which the user arrives after an instruction has been given, and before another one is requested. Nine destinations within the city of Edinburgh were selected to be the tasks to complete (the task is to arrive to each destination, from a common starting point, see Figure 2). Each pair of DG and DF had to complete all tasks and record their progress.

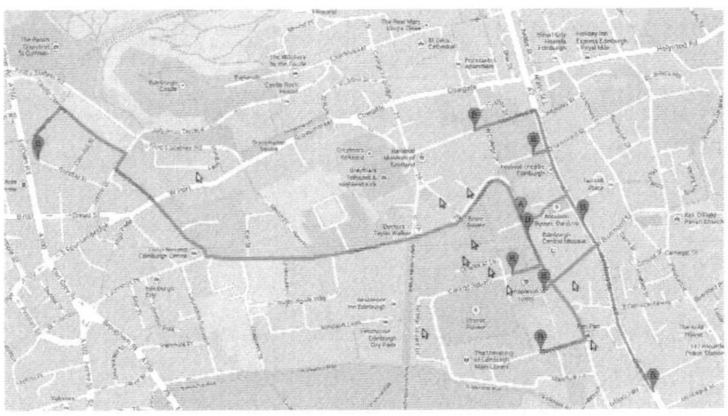

Figure 2: The 9 selected tasks .

For the creation of the corpus, a slightly modified version of the GRUVE wizards-desk was used. This tool is connected to the GRUVE web-client, and allows a human user to act as DF, generating instructions to assist the user in the completion of the task and monitoring his progression. Each instruction generated by a DG was numbered in order, in relation to each task. For example: if the fifth instruction given by the third DG, while performing the second task, was "Go forward and cross the square", then that instruction was numbered as follows:

$$5.3.2 - "Go\ forward\ and\ cross\ the\ square".$$

This notation was included to maintain the generation order between instructions (as the tasks were given in an arbitrary specific order for each DG). With **last-generated**, we refer to the instructions that were generated in the last 3 runs of each DG. This notion is needed to evaluate the effect of the increasing knowledge of the city (this metric is explained in Section 4).

As discussed in (Benotti and Denis, 2011) misinterpreted instructions and corrections result in clearly inappropriate instruction-reaction associations. Since we want to avoid any manual annotation, but we also want to minimize the quantity of errors inside the corpus, we decided to create a first corpus in which the same person portraits the roles of DG and DF. This allows us to eliminate the ambiguity of the instruction interpretation on the DF side, and eliminates correction instructions (instructions that are of no use for guidance, but were made to correct a previous error from the DG, or a wrong action from the DF). Later on, each instruction in this corpus was performed upon the virtual world by various others users, their reactions compared to the original reaction, and scored. For each task, only the instructions whose score exceeded an acceptance threshold remained in the final corpus.

3.2 Instruction selection

The instruction selection algorithm, displayed in Algorithm 1 consists in finding in the corpus the set of candidate utterances C for the current task plan P, which is the sequence of actions that needs to be executed in the current state of the virtual world in order to complete the task. We use the planner included in GRUVE to create P. We define:

$$C = \{U \in Corpus \mid P\ starts\ with\ U.Reaction\}$$

In other words, an utterance U belongs to C if the first action of the current plan P exactly matches the reaction associated to the utterance U. Whenever the plan P changes, as a result of the actions of the DF, we call the selection algorithm in order to regenerate the set of candidate utterances C.

Algorithm 1 Selection Algorithm

$C \leftarrow \emptyset$
$action \leftarrow nextAction(currentObjective)$
for all $Utterance\ U \in Corpus$ **do**
  if $action = U.Reaction$ **then**
    $C \leftarrow C \cup U$
  end if
end for

All the utterances that pass this test are considered paraphrases and hence suitable in the current context. Given a set of candidate paraphrases, one has to consider two cases: the most frequent case when there are several candidates and the possible case when there is no candidate.

- No candidate available: If no instruction is selected because the current plan cannot be matched with any existing reaction, a default, neutral, instruction "go" is uttered.
- Multiple candidates available: When multiple paraphrases are available, the agent must select one to transmit to the user. In this case, the algorithm selects one from the set of the last-generated instructions for the task (see Section 3.1).

4 Evaluation and expected results

Is this section we present the metrics and evaluation process that will be performed to test the virtual instructor presented in Section 3, which was generated using the dialogue model algorithm introduced in Section 3.2.

4.1 Objective metrics

The objective metrics are summarized below:

- Task success: successful runs.
- Canceled: runs not finished.
- Lost: runs finished but failed.
- Time (sec): average for successful runs.
- Utterances: average per successful run.

With this metrics, we will compare 3 systems: agents A, B and C.

Agent A is the GRUVE buddy system, which is provider by the GRUVE Challenge organizers as a baseline. Agent B consists of our virtual instructor, configured to select a random instruction when presented with multiple candidates (see Section 3.1). Agent C is also our virtual instructor, but when presented with several candidates, C selects a candidate who is also part of the last-generated set. As each task was completed in different order by each DG when the corpus was created, it is expected that in every set of candidates, the most late-generated instructions were created with greater knowledge of the city.

4.2 Subjective metrics

The subjective measures will be obtained from responses to a questionnaire given to each user at the end of the evaluation, based partially on the GIVE-2 Challenge questionnaire (Koller et al., 2010). It ask users to rate different statements about the system using a 0 *to* 10 scale.

The questionnaire will include 19 subjective metrics presented below:

Q1: *The system used words and phrases that were easy to understand.*

Q2: *I had to re-read instructions to understand what I needed to do.*

Q3: *The system gave me useful feedback about my progress.*

Q4: *I was confused about what to do next.*

Q5: *I was confused about which direction to go in.*

Q6: *I had no difficulty with identifying the objects the system described for me.*

Q7: *The system gave me a lot of unnecessary Information.*

Q8: *The system gave me too much information all at once.*

Q9: *The system immediately offered help when I was in trouble.*

Q10: *The system sent instructions too late.*

Q11: *The systems instructions were delivered too early.*

Q12: *The systems instructions were clearly worded.*

Q13: *The systems instructions sounded robotic.*

Q14: *The systems instructions were repetitive.*

Q15: *I lost track of time while solving the overall task.*

Q16: *I enjoyed solving the overall task.*

Q17: *Interacting with the system was really annoying.*

Q18: *The system was very friendly.*

Q19: *I felt I could trust the systems instructions.*

Metrics Q1 to Q12 assess the effectiveness and reliability of instructions, while metrics Q13 to Q19 are intended to assess the naturalness of the instructions, as well as the immersion and engagement of the interaction.

4.3 Expected results

Based on the results obtained by (Benotti and Denis, 2011) in the GIVE-2 Challenge, we expect a good rate of successful runs for the agent. Furthermore, the most interesting part of the evaluation resides in the comparison between agents B and C. We expect that the different selection methods of this agents, when presented with multiple instruction candidates, can provide information about the form in which the level of knowledge of the virtual world or environment modifies the capacity of a Direction Giver to create correct, and useful, instructions.

References

Luciana Benotti and Alexandre Denis. 2011. Giving instructions in virtual environments by corpus based selection. In *Proceedings of the SIGDIAL 2011 Conference*, SIGDIAL '11, pages 68–77. Association for Computational Linguistics.

D. Byron, A. Koller, J. Oberlander, L. Stoia, and K. Striegnitz. 2007. Generating instructions in virtual environments (give): A challenge and evaluation testbed for nlg. In *Proceedings of the Workshop on Shared Tasks and Comparative Evaluation in Natural Language Generation*.

Frank Dignum. 2012. Agents for games and simulations. *Autonomous Agents and Multi-Agent Systems*, 24(2):217–220, March.

S. Gandhe and D. Traum. 2007. First steps toward dialogue modelling from an un-annotated human-human corpus. In *IJCAI Workshop on Knowledge and Reasoning in Practical Dialogue Systemss*.

Dusan Jan, Antonio Roque, Anton Leuski, Jacki Morie, and David Traum. 2009. A virtual tour guide for virtual worlds. In *Proceedings of the 9th International Conference on Intelligent Virtual Agents*, IVA '09, pages 372–378, Berlin, Heidelberg. Springer-Verlag.

Srinivasan Janarthanam, Oliver Lemon, and Xingkun Liu. 2012. A web-based evaluation framework for spatial instruction-giving systems. In *Proceedings of the ACL 2012 System Demonstrations*, ACL '12, pages 49–54. Association for Computational Linguistics.

Patrick Kenny, Thomas D. Parsons, Jonathan Gratch, Anton Leuski, and Albert A. Rizzo. 2007. Virtual patients for clinical therapist skills training. In *Proceedings of the 7th International Conference on Intelligent Virtual Agents*, IVA '07, pages 197–210, Berlin, Heidelberg. Springer-Verlag.

Julia M. Kim, Randall W. Hill, Jr., Paula J. Durlach, H. Chad Lane, Eric Forbell, Mark Core, Stacy Marsella, David Pynadath, and John Hart. 2009. Bilat: A game-based environment for practicing negotiation in a cultural context. *Int. J. Artif. Intell. Ed.*, 19(3):289–308, August.

A. Koller, J. Moore, B. Eugenio, J. Lester, L. Stoia, D. Byron, J. Oberlander, and K. Striegnitz. 2007. Shared task proposal: Instruction giving in virtual worlds. In *In Workshop on Shared Tasks and Comparative Evaluation in Natural Language Generation.*

Alexander Koller, Kristina Striegnitz, Andrew Gargett, Donna Byron, Justine Cassell, Robert Dale, Johanna Moore, and Jon Oberlander. 2010. Report on the second nlg challenge on generating instructions in virtual environments (give-2). In *Proceedings of the 6th International Natural Language Generation Conference*, INLG '10, pages 243–250. Association for Computational Linguistics.

Anton Leuski, Ronakkumar Patel, David Traum, and Brandon Kennedy. 2006. Building effective question answering characters. In *Proceedings of the 7th SIGdial Workshop on Discourse and Dialogue*, SigDIAL '06, pages 18–27. Association for Computational Linguistics.

David Nunan. 2004. *Task-based language teaching*. University Press, Cambridge.

B.A. Shawar and E. Atwell. 2003. Using dialogue corpora to retrain a chatbot system. In *Proceedings of the Corpus Linguistics Conference*, pages 681–690.

B.A. Shawar and E. Atwell. 2005. Using corpora in machine-learning chatbot systems. *International Journal of Corpus Linguistics*, 10:489–516.

Mining human interactions to construct a virtual guide for a virtual fair

Andrés Luna
LIIS Group, FaMAF
Universidad Nacional de Córdoba
Córdoba, Argentina
andres.ignacio.luna@gmail.com

Luciana Benotti
LIIS Group, FaMAF
Universidad Nacional de Córdoba
Córdoba, Argentina
luciana.benotti@gmail.com

Abstract

In this paper we describe how we mine interactions between a human guide and a human visitor to build a virtual guide. A virtual guide is an agent capable of fulfilling the role of a human guide. Its goal is to guide visitors to each booth of a virtual fair and to provide information about the company or organization through interactive objects located at the fair.

The guide decides what to say, using a graph search algorithm, and decides how to say using generation by selection based on contextual features. The guide decides where to speak at the virtual fair by creating clusters using a data classification algorithm to learn in what positions the human guide decided to talk.

1 Introduction and previous work

Fairs are spaces where companies that offer similar products and services meet to promote them. A virtual fair emulates a real fair and can be available before the real fair happens in order to promote it to its potential visitors.

The virtual fair used in this work is a tourism fair that took place in Mexico, where visitors could find in each company's booth interactive video and links to tourist companies' websites promoting particular products. The goal of the virtual guide is to walk the user through the virtual fair, providing information about the companies' booths and inviting them to click on interactive objects to obtain more information.

In (Jan et al., 2009) the authors describe a virtual guide used to promote an island in the online game *Second Life* whose goal was to provide information to US army veterans. Our approach differs to that of (Jan et al., 2009) in that the virtual guide learns where to speak and how to realize its contributions from an automatically annotated corpus, rather than by using manually designed rules. However, our guide is not able to interpret utterances from the visitor, its decisions are only based on the visitor behavior. Natural language generation is achieved by adapting the *generation by selection* method described in (Benotti and Denis, 2011a; Benotti and Denis, 2011b).

The generation by selection method affords the use of complex and human-like sentences, and it does not need rule writing by a dialogue expert or manual annotations, among other of their many advantages. The disadvantage of corpus based generation is that the resulting dialogue may not be fully coherent. Shawar and Atwell (2003; 2005) present a method for learning pattern matching rules from corpora in order to obtain the dialogue manager for a chatbot. Gandhe and Traum (2007a; 2007b) investigate several dialogue models for negotiating virtual agents that are trained on an unannotated human-human corpus. Both approaches report that the dialogues obtained by these methods are still to be improved because the lack of dialogue history management results in incoherence. Since in task-based systems, the dialogue history is restricted by the structure of the task, the absence of dialogue history management is alleviated by tracking the current state of the task.

In Section 2 we introduce the corpus used by this work. We discuss the clustering method used on the corpus in Section 3; the clustering is used to decide where to speak. After that, we describe in Section 4 the mechanisms for instruction generation and graph search used to guide the visitors. Later, in Section 5 we show the results obtained in the evaluation process and compare our system's performance with other virtual instructors. Finally, in Section 6 we elaborate a conclusion about the virtual guide performance and capabilities, as well as discuss the possible improvements.

2 Virtual guide human-human corpus

We collected a corpus using a human guide in a wizard of Oz setup (Kelley, 1983). The corpus is comprised by 5 correct sessions in total performed by the same virtual tour guide, and according to the desired behavior and actions as specified for both participants. We recorded 2 hours and 2 minutes of virtual fair guided visits which produced a total of 136 utterances, having employed 18.02 words and 89.29 characters in average per utterance. 9 different interactive objects were clicked located in 4 different booths in average per session. In Figure 1 we show an aerial view of the virtual fair and the occurrence of utterances, marked in blue.

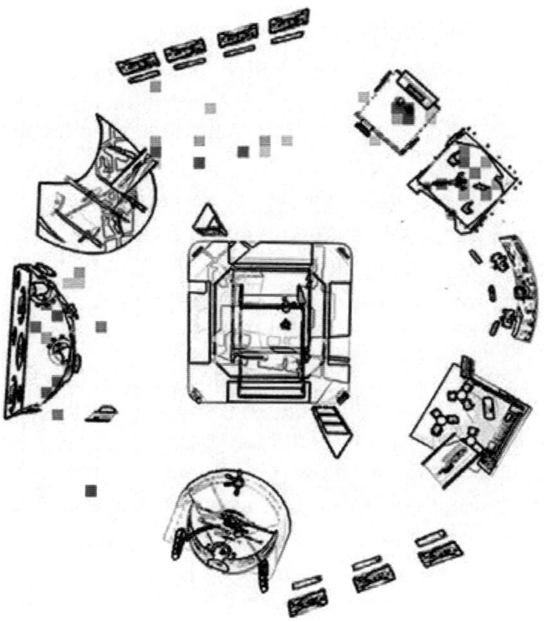

Figure 1: Map of registered utterances in corpus. A higher color intensity denotes a higher utterance density in the area.

3 Behavior-based utterance clustering

The generation by selection method that we use in this work is based on contextual features, in particular it is based on the position of the visitor inside the virtual fair and the actions that are affordable from that region in the fair. Deciding whether two positions in the fair have the same affordances, or, as we call it, fall into the same region is critical to select appropriate utterances from the corpus depending on the guide's location and task progress.

The discretization employed in (Benotti and Denis, 2011a) was geometrical discretization, dividing the world in regions based on the area visible to the guide. Instead of doing a geometrical discretization our virtual fair discretization was behavior-oriented which means that regions are delimited by clustering utterances that were uttered in a close position from each other. In the corpus utterances tend to cluster around *decision points*, locations there is more than one affordable and salient action available to the user and when the help and direction of the guide is required.

Geometrical region identification based on visibility normally requires a larger corpus in order to get a correct utterance generation, because the chance of having a region without any utterance occurrence inside is higher. In such discretization, different regions may contain a very different number of utterances while using behavior-oriented discretization results in regions with a similar number of utterances each. That is why the behavior-oriented discretization is an advantage for our virtual guide, since our corpus is considerably smaller to that used in (Benotti and Denis, 2011a).

We ran a modified version of the *k-means clustering* algorithm (Pakhira, 2009) that avoids empty clusters over our corpus to group instructions. As paraphrase instructions, while performing a task, occur in a same decision point, then we wanted close instructions to be in the same cluster, and therefore our criteria of "similarity" between them was euclidean distance. Ideally, different decision points should be in different clusters to guarantee selected utterances are appropriate in every situation.

Let us visualize virtual fair as a directed graph (V, E) where $V = regions$, and if $a, b \in V$ then $(a, b) \in E$ if and only if there is at least one utterance in the corpus whose immediate reaction was moving from region a to the region b. If we choose a low number of clusters the k-means clustering algorithm would cluster instructions of different nature, and conversely a too high value would make the virtual fair disconnected. Then, to obtain an optimal clustering -and therefore an optimal discretization- we maximize the k parameter such that the virtual fair's graph is still connected.

Discretization is finally obtained by matching every position (x, y) in the environment to the nearest cluster's *centroid*. We show in Figure 2 the virtual fair discretized in $k = 22$ regions, as that number was the maximum number of clusters we could reach without breaking the graph connectivity. Regions are delimited by lines and centroids are represented by white squares.

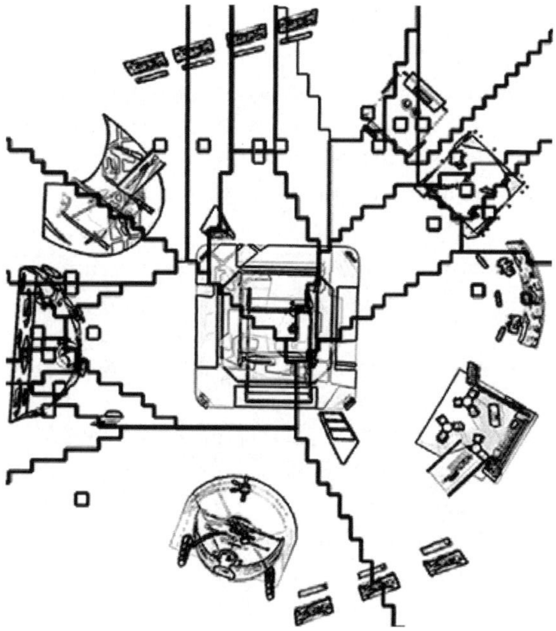

Figure 2: Virtual fair divided in $k = 22$ regions

4 The virtual guide

The virtual guide must direct visitors through the fair to interactive objects in order to complete its promotion duty in each visit session. We show in Figure 3 a situation in which a visitor is near an interactive object and the virtual guide encourages him/her to click it generating an utterance whose translation is *"If you click on the green cube you will access Lawson's website where you can learn more about them and the communication services they offer"*.

We can see the use of a referring expression, a negative politeness strategy (Brown and Levinson, 1987) to suggest an action but not impose it while some information about the Lawson firm is given.

In subsection 4.1 we discuss about the corpus automatic annotation. Then we describe how utterances are selected in subsection 4.2.

4.1 Corpus annotation

Our annotation process was simpler and more straightforward than (Benotti and Denis, 2011a), where artificial intelligence planning is used to normalize reactions, mainly due to the fact that users can not change the virtual fair state during their visit, they can only change their own posi-

Figure 3: The virtual guide took the visitor to an interactive object and encourages him/her to manipulate it

tion and visibility area (defined by the orientation in the virtual fair) and manipulate interactive objects.

In a virtual fair visit, the set of user's relevant actions are:

- Move from one region to another
- Change orientation to left or right
- Click on an interactive object

Consequently, the set of atoms representing a virtual fair's state was simplified to

- *user-region(region)*
- *user-orientation(x,y,z,w)* [1]
- *clicked(anInteractiveObject)*

In short, to do automatic annotation on the virtual guide's corpus, it was sufficient to observe the subsequent action to each utterance by looking for a change on any of the atoms shown above, and annotating and associating the corresponding reaction to the utterance and the valid atoms set when it was said.

4.2 Selecting what to say

The virtual guide's goal is to make the visitor visit a number of given objectives, namely a set of stands and interactive objects. Using the virtual fairs discretization and taking the directed graph representation we presented in Section 3, the virtual guide uses the A* algorithm to obtain a path, that is a sequence of actions, from its current position to the region where the next objective is located. In case the visitor got lost or simply took an alternative path, the virtual guide recalculates the shortest path and proceeds to guide the visitor through it.

[1] In quaternion representation

Clearly, in order to do this calculation it is critical that every objective is reachable from any node in the graph, so choosing a k parameter in the discretization process must be done taking care of that.

The virtual guide gives the visitor a new instruction depending on next actions to perform using the selection algorithm taken from (Benotti and Denis, 2011a), shown in Algorithm 1. The algorithm obtains set of utterances C, all of which have a reaction that corresponds to the sequence of actions that the virtual guide wants the visitor to perform next.

Algorithm 1 Virtual guide's selection algorithm

```
C ← ∅
action ← nextAction(currentObjective)
for all Utterance U ∈ Corpus do
  if action ≈ U.Reaction then
    C ← C ∪ U
  end if
end for
```

5 Evaluation results

In the evaluation process 11 evaluators participated, completing the proposed visit to the virtual fair, each manipulating 9 interactive objects. Evaluators were also asked to complete a questionnaire after the tour, in which we wanted to obtain several subjective metrics. We were particularly interested in the questions

- **S1**: *I had difficulties identifying the objects that the system described for me*
- **S2**: *The Utterances sounded robotic*
- **S3**: *The system was repetitive*

where we previously supposed the virtual guide would have better results than other virtual instructors, if we consider the results showed in (Benotti and Denis, 2011a).

We compared our virtual guide results with the two best symbolic systems built for another virtual environment, the GIVE-2 Challenge. Those systems were NA from INRIA and SAAR from University of Saarland (see (Koller et al., 2010)). Furthermore, we checked if the virtual guide results were similar to another virtual instructor, also built for GIVE-2, called OUR, in which generation by selection was applied to make natural language generation possible.

In Table 1 we show the results for each virtual instructor in the three categories we are interested. We can see that the virtual guide obtained significantly better results than the SAAR and NA and in questions **S1**, **S2** and **S3**, as we had supposed. All three questions range from 1 (one) to 9 (nine), the lower the number the better the system (since questions are negative).

Table 1: Results comparison between virtual guide and three GIVE-2 systems

Question	NA	SAAR	OUR	VP
S1	4.1	4	3	1.81
S2	5.2	4.75	3.6	1.82
S3	6.55	6.3	5.4	2

6 Conclusions and future work

In this paper we described the construction of a virtual guide for a virtual fair with the purpose of guiding visitors through the stands and to interactive objects located inside the fair. Inmersive virtual fairs and expositions constitute a promising way to promote such events.

On our evaluation, the virtual guide had comparable results than the virtual instructor GIVE-2 implemented using generation by selection, using a much smaller corpus. Our guide got better results that the two best performing symbolic systems. These results are preliminary, but also encouraging.

A possible extension of this work could be that virtual guide can continue to improve its behavior by learning online when input from a human guide of the fair is available. If more corpus is available in this way the virtual guide could discard those utterances that do not lead most visitors to perform the intended reaction.

As a result of this work we conclude that virtual guide met the basic functions of navigation and natural language generation that we expected and that the resulting prototype is ready to be deployed at the virtualization of events website `http://www.inixiavf.com/`.

References

Luciana Benotti and Alexandre Denis. 2011a. Giving instructions in virtual environments by corpus based selection. In *Proceedings of the SIGDIAL 2011*

Conference, SIGDIAL '11, pages 68–77, Stroudsburg, PA, USA. Association for Computational Linguistics.

Luciana Benotti and Alexandre Denis. 2011b. Prototyping virtual instructors from human-human corpora. In *Proceedings of the ACL-HLT 2011 System Demonstrations*, pages 62–67, Portland, Oregon, June. Association for Computational Linguistics.

Penelope Brown and Stephen Levinson. 1987. *Politeness: Some Universals in Language Usage*. Studies in Interactional Sociolinguistics. Cambridge University Press.

Sudeep Gandhe and David Traum. 2007a. Creating spoken dialogue characters from corpora without annotations. In *Proceedings of 8th Conference in the Annual Series of Interspeech Events*, pages 2201–2204, Belgium.

Sudeep Gandhe and David Traum. 2007b. First steps toward dialogue modelling from an un-annotated human-human corpus. In *IJCAI Workshop on Knowledge and Reasoning in Practical Dialogue Systems*, Hyderabad, India.

Dusan Jan, Antonio Roque, Anton Leuski, Jacki Morie, and David Traum. 2009. A virtual tour guide for virtual worlds. In *Proceedings of the 9th International Conference on Intelligent Virtual Agents*, IVA '09, pages 372–378, Berlin, Heidelberg. Springer-Verlag.

John F. Kelley. 1983. An empirical methodology for writing user-friendly natural language computer applications. In *Proceedings of the SIGCHI Conference on Human Factors in Computing Systems*, CHI '83, pages 193–196, New York, NY, USA. ACM.

Alexander Koller, Kristina Striegnitz, Andrew Gargett, Donna Byron, Justine Cassell, Robert Dale, Johanna Moore, and Jon Oberlander. 2010. Report on the second nlg challenge on generating instructions in virtual environments (give-2). In *Proceedings of the 6th International Natural Language Generation Conference*, INLG '10, pages 243–250, Stroudsburg, PA, USA. Association for Computational Linguistics.

Malay K. Pakhira. 2009. A modified k-means algorithm to avoid empty clusters. *International Journal of Recent Trends in Engineering*, 1(1):220–226.

Bayan Abu Shawar and Eric Atwell. 2003. Using dialogue corpora to retrain a chatbot system. In *Proceedings of the Corpus Linguistics Conference*, pages 681–690, United Kingdom.

Bayan Abu Shawar and Eric Atwell. 2005. Using corpora in machine-learning chatbot systems. volume 10, pages 489–516.

Collaborative Exploration in Human-Robot Teams: What's in Their Corpora of Dialog, Video, & LIDAR Messages?

Clare R. Voss* **Taylor Cassidy†*** **Douglas Summers-Stay***

*Army Research Laboratory, Adelphi, MD 20783

†IBM T. J. Watson Research Center, Hawthorne, NY 10532

{clare.r.voss.civ,taylor.cassidy.ctr,douglas.a.summers-stay.civ}@mail.mil

Abstract

This paper briefly sketches new work-in-progress (i) developing task-based scenarios where human-robot teams collaboratively explore real-world environments in which the robot is immersed but the humans are not, (ii) extracting and constructing "multi-modal interval corpora" from dialog, video, and LIDAR messages that were recorded in *ROS bagfiles* during task sessions, and (iii) testing automated methods to identify, track, and align co-referent content both within and across modalities in these interval corpora. The pre-pilot study and its corpora provide a unique, empirical starting point for our longer-term research objective: characterizing the balance of explicitly shared and tacitly assumed information exchanged during effective teamwork.

1 Overview

Robots that are able to move into areas where people cannot during emergencies and collaboratively explore these environments by teaming with humans, have tremendous potential to impact search and rescue operations. For human-robot teams to conduct such shared missions, humans need to trust that they will be kept apprised, at a miniumum, of where the robot is and what it is sensing, as it moves about without them present.

Figure 1: Outside View: Video Image & LIDAR.

To begin documenting the communication challenges humans face in taking a robot's perspective, we conducted a *pre-pilot* study[1] to record, identify and track the dialog, video, and LIDAR information that is explicitly shared by, or indirectly available to, members of human-robot teams when conducting collaborative tasks.

1.1 Approach

We enlisted colleagues to be the commander (C) or the human (R) controlling a mobile physical robot in such tasks. Neither could see the robot. Only R could "see for" the robot, via its onboard video camera and LIDAR. C and R communicated by text chat on their computers, as in this example,

R_41: I can see in the entrance.
C_42: Enter and scan the first room.

R_44: I see a door to the right and a door to the left.
C_45: Scan next open room on left.

Utterances R_41 & C_42 occur when the robot is outdoors (Fig. 1) and R_44 & C_45 occur after it moves indoors (Fig. 2). Although our approach resembles a *Wizard* **and** *Oz* paradigm (Riek, 2012),

[1] Statisticians say *pre-pilots* are for "kicking the tires," early-stage tests of scenarios, equipment, and data collection.

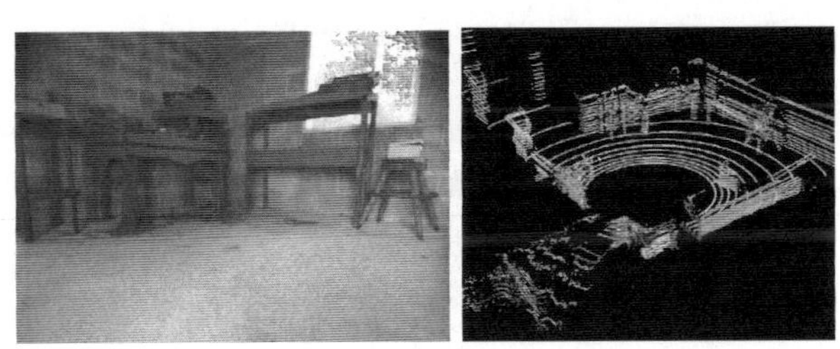

Figure 2: Inside View: Video Image & LIDAR. *Brightness and contrast of video image increased for print publication.*

with C as User and R as Wizard controlling the robot, there is no intent for R to deceive C.

In these dialog snippets, notice that the doors mentioned in R_44 are not visible in the image of that utterance's time interval and, even if they had been visible, their referents were context-dependent and ambiguous. How are the robot and human to refer to the same door? This challenge entails resolving several types of co-reference (linguistic, are they talking about the same door? visual, are they looking at the door? navigational, is one backing into a door no longer in view but previosuly stored in its map?) Successful communication on human-robot teams, *where humans send messages to direct robot movements and receive robot-processed messages as the robot navigates,* entails effective identification of named referents (such as doors), both within and across available modalities during exploratory tasks. The research question is, how might the identification and alignment of entities using combinations of (i) NLP on dialog, (ii) image processing on the video and LIDAR stream, with (iii) robot position, motion, and orientation coordinates, support more effective human-robot missions?

We conducted the pre-pilot study with ten trial sessions to collect multi-modal data from C-R and R-only scenarios (Table 1). Each session involved a single participant playing the role of R with control over the physical robot, or two participants, one person playing R and one playing C.

Team	R's Task
R only	Rotate in place and describe surroundings.
R only	Move along road, describe surroundings.
C, R	Follow C's guidance in navigating building's perimeter, describe surroundings.
C, R	Follow C's guidance in searching buildings for specified objects.

Table 1: Pre-pilot Scenarios.

Participants sat indoors and could not see the robot outside, roughly 30 meters away. In each session, R was instructed to act as though he or she were situated in the robot's position and to obey C. R was to consider the robot's actions as R's own, and to consider available video and LIDAR point cloud feeds as R's own perceptions.

1.2 Equipment

All participants worked from their own computers. Each was instructed, for a given scenario, to be either C or R and to communicate by text only. On their screen they saw a dedicated dialog (chat) window in a Linux terminal. For sessions with both C and R, the same dialog content (the ongoing sequence of typed-in utterances) appeared in the dialog window on each of their screens.

The physical robot ran under the Robot Operating System (ROS) (Quigley et al., 2009), equipped with a video camera, laser sensors, magnetometer, GPS unit, and rotary encoders. R could "see for the robot" via two ROS *rviz* windows with live feeds for video from the robot's camera and constructed 3D point cloud frames.[2] R had access to rotate and zoom functions to alter the screen display of the point cloud. C saw only a static bird's-eye-view map of the area. R remotely controlled over a network connection the robot's four wheels and its motion, using the left joystick of an X-Box controller.

1.3 Collection

During each session, all data from the robot's sensors and dialog window was recorded via the *rosbag* tool and stored in a single *bagfile*.[3] A bagfile contains typed *messages*. Each message contains a timestamp (specified at nanosecond granularity) and values for that message type's attributes. Message types *geometry_msgs/PoseStamped*, for example, contain a time stamp, a three-dimensional location vector and a four-dimensional orientation vector that indicates an estimate of the robot's location and the direction in which it is facing. The robot's rotary encoders generate these messages as the robot moves. The primary bagfile message types most relevant to our initial analyses[4] were:

1) instant_messenger/StringStamped
that included speaker id, text utterances
2) sensor_msgs/PointCloud2
that included LIDAR data
3) sensor_msgs/CompressedImage
with compressed, rectified video images
4) sensor_msgs/GPS, with robot coordinates

Message types are packaged and *published* at different rates: some are published automatically at regular intervals (e.g., image frames), while others depend on R, C, or robot activity (e.g., dialog utterances). And the specific rate of publication for some message types can be limited at times by network bandwidth constraints (e.g. LIDAR data). Summary statistics for our initial pre-pilot collec-

[2]LIDAR measures distance from robot by illuminating targets with robot lasers and generates point cloud messages.

[3]http://wiki.ros.org/rosbag

[4]We omit here details of ROS *topics*, *transformation messages*, and other sensor data collected in the pre-pilot.

tion consisting of ten task sessions conducted over two days, and that together spanned roughly five hours in real-time, are presented in Table 2.

#bagfile msgs	$15,131K$	#dialog utts	434
min per sn	$140,848$	min per sn	15
max per sn	$3,030K$	max per sn	116
#tokens	$3,750$	#image msgs	$10,650$
min per sn	200	min per sn	417
max per sn	793	max per sn	$1,894$
#unique words	568	#LIDAR msgs	$8,422$
min per sn	84	min per sn	215
max per sn	176	max per sn	$2,250$

Table 2: Collection Statistics (sn = session).

2 From Collection to Interval Corpora

After collecting millions of messages in the pre-pilot with content in different modalities, the immediate research challenge has been identifying the time interval that covers the messages directly related to the content in each utterance.

We extracted each utterance message u and its corresponding time stamp t. For a given u, we extracted the five image, five point cloud, and five GPS messages immediately preceding and the five of each immediately following u, based on message time-stamps, for a total of thirty sensor messages per utterance. These message types were published independent of the robot's movement, approximately once per second. In the second phase, we assigned the earliest and latest time stamp from the first-phase messages to delimit an interval $[t_s, t_e]$ and conducted another extraction round from the bagfile, this time pulling out all messages with time stamps in that interval as published by the rotary encoders, compass, and inertial measurement unit, only when the robot moved. The messages from both phases constitute a ten-second *interval corpus* for u.

These interval corpora serve as a first approximation at segmenting the massive stream published at nanosecond-level into units pertaining to commander-robot dialog during the task at hand. With manual inspection, we found that many automatically-constructed intervals do track relevant changes in the robot's location. For example, the latest interval in a task's time sequence that was constructed with the robot being outside a building is distinct from the first interval that covers when the robot moves inside the building.[5]

[5]This appears likely due to the paced descriptions in R's utterances. Another pre-pilot is needed to test this hypothesis.

3 Corpora Language Processing

Each utterance collected from the sessions was tokenized, parsed, and semantically interpreted using SLURP (Brooks et al., 2012), a well-tested NLP front-end component of a human-robot system.[6] The progression in SLURP's analysis pipeline for utterance C_45 is shown in Figure 3.

SLURP extracts a parse tree (top-left), identifies a sub-tree that constitutes a verb-argument structure, and enumerates possibly matching sense-specific *verb frames* from VerbNet (Schuler, 2005) (bottom-left). VerbNet provides a syntactic to semantic role mapping for each frame (top-right). SLURP selects the best mapping and generates a compact semantic representation (bottom-right).[7] In this example, the correct sense of "scan" is selected (*investigate-35.4*) along with a frame that matches the syntactic parse. Overall, half the commands run through SLURP generated a semantic interpretation. Of the other half, roughly one quarter failed or had errors at parsing and the other quarter at the argument matching stage.

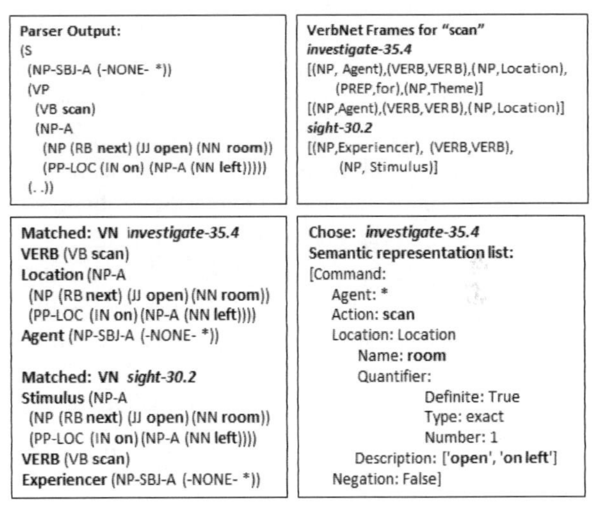

Figure 3: Analyses of *Scan next open room on left.*

Our next step is to augment SLURP's lexicon and retrain a parser for new vocabulary so that we can directly map semantic structures of the pre-pilot corpora into ResearchCyc[8], an extensive ontology, for cross-reference to other events and objects, already stored and possibly originated as visual input. Following McFate (2010), we will test

[6]https://github.com/PennNLP/SLURP.

[7]Verbnet associates each frame with a conjunction of boolean semantic predicates that specify how and when event participants interact, for an event variable (not shown).

[8]ResearchCyc and CycL are trademarks of Cycorp, Inc.

Figure 4: Outside View: Image, Zones, Overlay

Figure 5: Inside View: Image, Zones, Overlay. *Brightness and contrast of video image and overlay increased for print publication.*

the mapping of matched VerbNet frames to ResearchCyc's semantic predicates to assess its lexical coverage for our corpora.

4 Image Processing

Interval corpus images were labelled by a neural network trained for visual scene classification (Munoz, 2013) of nine material classes: dirt, foliage, grass, road, sidewalk, sky, wall, wood, and ground cover (organic debris). Figures 4 and 5 show the images from Figures 1 and 2 with two additional versions: one with colored zones for system-recognized class boundaries and another with colored zones as trasparent overlays on the original. The classes differentiate terrain types that work well with route-finding techniques that leverage them in selecting traversible paths. As the robot systems are enhanced with more sophisticated path planning software, that knowledge may be combined with recognized zones to send team members messages about navigation problems as the robot explores where they cannot go.

Accuracy is limited at the single image level: the actual grass in Figure 4 is mostly mis-classified as *dirt* (blue) along with some correctly identified *grass* (green), while the floor in Figure 5 is misclassified as *road,* although much of what shows through the window is correctly classified as *foliage.* We are experimenting with automatically assigning natural language (NL) labels to a range of objects and textures recognized in images from other larger datasets. We can retrieve labeled images stored in ResearchCyc via NL query converted into CycL, allowing a commander to, for example, ask questions about objects and regions using terms related to but not necessarily equal to the original recognition system-provided labels.

5 Related Work

We are aware of no other multi-modal corpora obtained from human-robot teams conducting exploratory missions with collected dialog, video and other sensor data. Corpora with a robot recording similar data modalities do exist (Green et al., 2006; Wienke et al., 2012; Maas et al., 2006) but for fundamentally different tasks. Tellex et al. (2011) and Matuszek et al. (2012) pair commands with formal plans without dialog and Zender et al. (2008) and Randelli et al. (2013) build multi-level maps but with a situated commander.

Eberhard et al. (2010)'s CReST corpus contains a set-up similar to ours minus the robot; a human task-solver wears a forward-facing camera instead. The SCARE corpus (Stoia et al., 2008) records similar modalities but in a virtual environment, where C has full access to R's video feed. Other projects yielded corpora from virtual environments that include route descriptions without dialog (Marge and Rudnicky, 2011; MacMahon et al., 2006; Vogel and Jurafsky, 2010) or referring expressions without routes (Schütte et al., 2010; Fang et al., 2013), assuming pre-existing abstractions from sensor data.

6 Conclusion and Ongoing Work

We have presented our pre-pilot study with data collection and corpus construction phases. This work-in-progress requires further analysis. We are now processing dialog utterances for more systematic semantic interpretation using disambiguated VerbNet frames that map into ResearchCyc predicates. We will run object recognition software retrained on a broader range of objects so that it can be applied to images that will be labelled and stored in ResearchCyc micro-worlds for subsequent co-reference with terms in the dialog utterances. Ultimately we want to establish in real time links across parts of messages in different modalities that refer to the same abstract entities, so that humans and robots can share their separately-obtained knowledge about the entities and their spatial relations — whether seen, sensed, described, or inferred — when communicating on shared tasks in environments.

Acknowledgments

Over a dozen engineers and researchers assisted us in many ways before, during, and after the prepilot, providing technical help with equipment and data collection, as well as participating in the prepilot. We cannot list everyone here, but special thanks to Stuart Young for providing clear guidance to everyone working with us.

References

Daniel J. Brooks, Constantine Lignos, Cameron Finucane, Mikhail S. Medvedev, Ian Perera, Vasumathi Raman, Hadas Kress-Gazit, Mitch Marcus, and Holly A. Yanco. 2012. Make it so: Continuous, flexible natural language interaction with an autonomous robot. In *Proc. AAAI*, pages 2–8.

Kathleen M. Eberhard, Hannele Nicholson, Sandra Kübler, Susan Gundersen, and Matthias Scheutz. 2010. The indiana "cooperative remote search task" (crest) corpus. In *Proc. LREC*.

Rui Fang, Changsong Liu, Lanbo She, and Joyce Y. Chai. 2013. Towards situated dialogue: Revisiting referring expression generation. In *Proc. EMNLP*, pages 392–402.

Anders Green, Helge Httenrauch, and Kerstin Severinson Eklundh. 2006. Developing a contextualized multimodal corpus for human-robot interaction. In *Proc. LREC*.

Jan F. Maas, Britta Wrede, and Gerhard Sagerer. 2006. Towards a multimodal topic tracking system for a mobile robot. In *Proc. INTERSPEECH*.

Matt MacMahon, Brian Stankiewicz, and Benjamin Kuipers. 2006. Walk the talk: Connecting language, knowledge, and action in route instructions. In *Proc. AAAI*, pages 1475–1482.

Matthew Marge and Alexander I Rudnicky. 2011. The teamtalk corpus: Route instructions in open spaces. In *Proc. RSS, Workshop on Grounding Human-Robot Dialog for Spatial Tasks*.

Cynthia Matuszek, Evan Herbst, Luke S. Zettlemoyer, and Dieter Fox. 2012. Learning to parse natural language commands to a robot control system. In *Proc. ISER*, pages 403–415.

Clifton McFate. 2010. Expanding verb coverage in cyc with verbnet. In *Proc. ACL, Student Research Workshop*, pages 61–66.

Daniel Munoz. 2013. *Inference Machines: Parsing Scenes via Iterated Predictions*. Ph.D. thesis, Carnegie Mellon University.

Morgan Quigley, Ken Conley, Brian Gerkey, Josh Faust, Tully B. Foote, Jeremy Leibs, Rob Wheeler, and Andrew Y. Ng. 2009. ROS: an open-source robot operating system. In *Proc. ICRA, Workshop on Open Source Software*.

Gabriele Randelli, Taigo Maria Bonanni, Luca Iocchi, and Daniele Nardi. 2013. Knowledge acquisition through human–robot multimodal interaction. *Intelligent Service Robotics*, 6(1):19–31.

Laurel D Riek. 2012. Wizard of oz studies in hri: A systematic review and new reporting guidelines. *Journal of Human-Robot Interaction*, 1(1).

Karin Kipper Schuler. 2005. *Verbnet: A Broad-coverage, Comprehensive Verb Lexicon*. Ph.D. thesis, University of Pennsylvania.

Niels Schütte, John D. Kelleher, and Brian Mac Namee. 2010. Visual salience and reference resolution in situated dialogues: A corpus-based evaluation. In *Proc. AAAI, Fall Symposium: Dialog with Robots*.

Laura Stoia, Darla Magdalena Shockley, Donna K. Byron, and Eric Fosler-Lussier. 2008. Scare: a situated corpus with annotated referring expressions. In *Proc. LREC*.

Stefanie Tellex, Thomas Kollar, Steven Dickerson, Matthew R. Walter, Ashis Gopal Banerjee, Seth J. Teller, and Nicholas Roy. 2011. Understanding natural language commands for robotic navigation and mobile manipulation. In *Proc. AAAI*.

Adam Vogel and Daniel Jurafsky. 2010. Learning to follow navigational directions. In *Proc. ACL*, pages 806–814.

Johannes Wienke, David Klotz, and Sebastian Wrede. 2012. A framework for the acquisition of multimodal human-robot interaction data sets with a whole-system perspective. In *Proc. LREC, Workshop on Multimodal Corpora for Machine Learning*.

Hendrik Zender, O Martínez Mozos, Patric Jensfelt, G-JM Kruijff, and Wolfram Burgard. 2008. Conceptual spatial representations for indoor mobile robots. *Robotics and Autonomous Systems*, 56(6):493–502.

Multi-threaded Interaction Management for Dynamic Spatial Applications

Srinivasan Janarthanam
Interaction Lab
Heriot-Watt University
Edinburgh
sc445@hw.ac.uk

Oliver Lemon
Interaction Lab
Heriot-Watt University
Edinburgh
o.lemon@hw.ac.uk

Abstract

We present a multi-threaded Interaction Manager (IM) that is used to track different dimensions of user-system conversations that are required to interleave with each other in a coherent and timely manner. This is explained in the context of a spoken dialogue system for pedestrian navigation and city question-answering, with information push about nearby or visible points-of-interest (PoI).

1 Introduction

We present a multi-threaded Interaction Manager (IM) that is used to track different dimensions of user-system conversations and interleave the different converational threads coherently. The IM that we present interacts with the user in a spatial domain and interleaves navigation information along with historical and cultural information about the entities that users can see around them. In addition, it aims to answer questions that users might have about those entities. This presents a complex conversational situation where several conversational threads have to be interleaved in such a way that the system utterances are presented to the user at the right time but in a prioritised order, and with bridging utterances when threads are interrupted and resumed. For instance, a navigation instruction may be important (since the user is walking up to a junction at which they need to turn) and therefore it needs to be spoken before continuing information presentation about an entity or answering other ongoing questions.

2 Related work

Previously, multi-threaded interaction was used to handle multiple simultaneous tasks in human-robot interaction (HRI) scenarios (Lemon and Gruenstein, 2004). This idea also turns out to be important for cases where humans are interacting with a variety of different web-services in parallel. Human multitasking in dialogue is discussed in (Yang et al., 2008).

(Lemon and Gruenstein, 2004) presented a multi-threaded dialogue management approach for managing several concurrent tasks in an HRI scenario. The robot could, for example be flying to a location while simultaneously searching for a vehicle, and utterances about both tasks could be interleaved. Here, conversational threads were managed using a representation called the "Dialogue Move Tree", which represented conversational threads as branches of the tree, linked to an "Activity Tree" which represented the states of ongoing robot tasks (deliver medical supplies, fly to a waypoint, search for a truck), which could be active simultaneously. The situation for our pedestrian navigation and information system is similar - concurrent tasks need to be managed coherently via conversation. The approach adopted in this paper is similar to (Lemon and Gruenstein, 2004). However, in this work we separate out a domain-general thread called 'dialogue control' which handles generic issues like clarification of reference across all tasks. This increasing modularisation of the dialogue threads makes it possible to learn individual dialogue policies for each one, in future work.

(Nakano et al., 2008) presented an approach where one of the several expert modules handling different tasks is activated based on the user input, but only one verbal expert is active at any one time. In contrast to this, we present an approach where several thread managers each handling a different task can be activated in parallel and their outputs stored and retrieved based on priority.

3 Multi-threaded IM

The Interaction Manager (IM) is the central component of any spoken dialogue system architec-

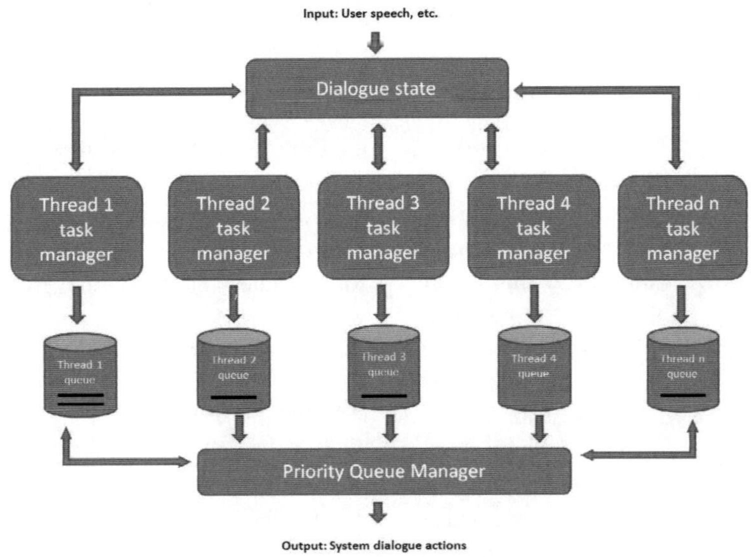

Figure 1: Interaction Manager Architecture

ture. Generally, it takes as input the user's utterances in the form of dialogue acts from the parser and identifies the next dialogue action to present to the user. Dialogue about a domain task is managed using a dialogue strategy or policy (e.g. (Young, 2000; Lemon and Pietquin, 2007)). A dialogue policy is a mapping between dialogue states and dialogue actions, which are semantic representations of what the system should say next.

In order to handle multiple tasks simultaneously, we present an architecture for a multi-threaded interaction manager that treats conversation about each domain task as a thread. These conversational threads are interleaved and managed using techniques such as multi-queuing, priority based pushing, and queue revision. We describe these techniques below. The architecture of the Interaction Manager is shown in figure 1.

Multi-threading and queuing
In order to manage complex interactions involving several conversational tasks/topics, we propose that the each task be handled by a thread manager within the interaction management framework. Each such manager will handle a conversational thread using a dialogue policy. Each thread manager will be fed with the input from the user and the dialogue actions generated will be stored in separate queues. This approach allows the interaction manager to produce several dialogue actions at the same time although for different conversational tasks.

Prioritised Queue Management
Dialogue actions from the several threads are stored in separate queues. The queues can be assigned priorities that decide the order in which items from the queues will be popped. The dialogue actions in the queues are pushed to the user based on an order of priority (see below). This priority can either be fixed or dynamic based on context. The system and user engagement should also be checked so that system utterances are pushed only when the system and user are not speaking already.

Queue Revision: resuming and bridging
The dialogue actions are generated and stored in queues. Therefore, there is a difference between the time they are generated and time that they are pushed. Therefore dialogue actions in the queues are revised periodically to reflect changes in context. Obsolete dialogue actions will have to removed for two reasons. Firstly, pushing them to the user may make the conversation incoherent because the system may be speaking about an entity that is no longer relevant and secondly, these obsolete dialogue actions may delay other other important dialogue actions from being pushed on time. In addition, it may also be useful to edit the dialogue actions to include discourse markers to signify topic change (Yang et al., 2008) and bridge

phrases to reintroduce a previous topic. We discuss some examples later in section 4.3.

4 SPACEBOOK Interaction Manager

As a part of the SpaceBook EU FP7 project, we implemented the above design for a multi-threaded interaction manager that presents the user with navigational instructions, pushes PoI information, and manages QA questions (Janarthanam et al., 2013). It receives the user's input in the form of a dialogue act (DA) from the ASR module and the user's location (latitude and longitude), orientation, and speed from the Pedestrian Tracker module. Based on these inputs and the dialogue context, the IM responds with a system output dialogue act. It should be noted that the location coordinates of the user are sent to the IM every 2 seconds. This allows the IM to generate location aware information at a high frequency. In addition, the IM has to deal with incoming requests and responses from the user's spoken inputs. With the possibility of system utterances being generated at a frequency of one every two seconds, there is a need for an efficient mechanism to manage the conversation and reduce the risk of overloading the user with information. These tasks are treated as separate conversational threads.

4.1 Conversational Threads

The SpaceBook IM manages the conversation using five conversational threads using dedicated task managers. Three threads: 'navigation', 'question answering' and 'PoI pushing', represent the core tasks of our system. In addition, for handling the issues in dialogue management, we introduce two threads: 'dialogue control' and 'request response'. These different threads represent the state of different dimensions of the user-system conversation that need to interleave with each other coherently. Each of the threads is managed by a thread manager using a dialogue policy. Each thread can generate a dialogue action depending on the context, as described below:

Dialogue Control

During the course of the conversation, the IM uses this thread to manage user requests for repetition, issues with unparsed (i.e. not understood) user utterances, utterances that have low ASR confidence, and so on. The dialogue control thread is also used to manage reference resolution in cases where referring expressions are underspecified. The IM resolves anaphoric references by keeping a record of entities mentioned in the dialogue context. It stores the name and type information for each entity (such as landmark, building, etc) mentioned in previous utterances by either user or system. Subsequent user references to these entities using expressions such as "the museum", "the cafe", and so on, are resolved by searching for the latest entity of the given type. In cases where the IM cannot resolve the referent, it asks the user to clarify.

Request Response

The user can also initiate tasks that interest him/her at anytime during the conversation. These tasks include searching for an entity (e.g. a museum or a restaurant), requesting navigation instructions to a destination, and asking questions about the entities in the city database such as their location ("Where is X?", "How far is X?"). During navigation, users might want to ask questions about the destination, ask for next instructions, etc. All these user requests are handled using the request response thread. For instance, when the user asks for directions, the IM resolves the destination entity (perhaps using clarification) in the city model and acknowledges the user request. The task is then further handled using the Navigation thread.

Navigation

The IM identifies the location of the destination entity and queries a city database (Bartie and Mackaness, 2013) for a route plan. Using the route plan, the navigation thread presents step-by-step instructions to the user based on the current location and orientation of the user. The IM continuously monitors users to determine if at any time they are deviating from the planned route and provides corrective instructions. As users get near to the next node on the route plan, the next instruction is given. The IM uses highly salient visible landmarks (Bartie et al., 2013) and popular landmarks near the nodes to instruct the user (e.g. "When you reach Clydesdale Bank, turn left on to Nicolson Square"). The IM also informs users when they pass by recognisable landmarks, just to reassure them that they are on the right track (e.g. "You will pass by Tesco on the right"). When the user is close to his/her destination, the IM determines whether the destination is visible to the user, informs the user, and closes the task.

Usr: I want to go to the National Gallery
Sys: Ok. I am now looking for directions to the National Gallery.
Sys: The National Gallery is on Queens Street at about 300 meters away.
....
Sys: Can you see the Bank of Scotland about 300 meters away on your left? It has a big green dome.
Usr: Yes. I can see it.
Sys: Walk towards it.
Sys: Can you see the National Gallery in front of you at about 100 meters? It is a building with Roman architecture.
Usr: Yes.
Sys: You have now reached your destination.

Question Answering

The system also answers ad hoc questions from the user (e.g. "Who is David Hume?", "What is the Old College?", "Who was William Wallace", etc). These are sent to the QA server and answered based on responses from the Question-Answering (QA) server (Janarthanam et al., 2013). The dialogue policy here is to answer the user's question with the first snippet available and ask the user to request for more if more snippets are available and he or she is interested.

Pushing PoI Information

When the user is mobile, the IM identifies popular points of interest (PoI) on the route based on two factors: proximity and visibility. The dialogue policy is to introduce the PoI, query the QA server for snippets and push the first snippet to the user. The user is encouraged to ask for more information if he/she is interested.

Sys: In front of you, about 200 meters away is Old College. It has a grey dome on top.
Sys: Situated on South Bridge, Old College is
. . .
Sys: Ask for more information if interested.

4.2 Priority assignment in SpaceBook

Priority is assigned to the above dialogue threads as follows:

Priority 1. Dialogue control (repeat request, clarifications etc)
Priority 2. Responding to user requests
Priority 3. System initiated navigation task actions
Priority 4. Responses to User-initiated QA actions
Priority 5. PoI Push actions

For instance, informing the user of a PoI could be delayed if the user needs to be given an instruction to turn at the junction he is approaching.

4.3 Queue revision and bridging utterances

The queues need to be revised at regular intervals in order to keep the information in them relevant to context. For instance, the dialogue action of informing the user of his/her location is deleted after 5 seconds, as this tends to become obsolete. Similarly, dialogue actions corresponding to information segments in PoI and QA queues are edited to inform the utterance generator of other intervening dialogue actions so that it can use appropriate bridge phrases to reintroduce the focus of the conversational thread. For instance, as shown in the example below, the utterance generator inserts a bridge phrase (i.e. "More on Old College") to reintroduce the focus of the PoI push task because of the intervening user request and the subsequent system response.

Sys: In front of you, about 200 meters away is the Old College. It has a grey dome on top.
User: Where am I?
Sys: You are on Chambers street.
Sys: **More on Old College**. Situated on South Bridge, the Old College is......

5 Conclusion

We presented an architecture for a multi-threaded Interaction Manager that can handle multiple conversational tasks. We also described an implementation of the architecture in a dynamic spatial environment. The SpaceBook IM is a multi-tasking IM that aims to interleave navigation information along with historical information about the entities users can see around them. In addition, it aims to answer questions users might have about those entities.

Acknowledgements

The research leading to these results has received funding from the European Community's Seventh Framework Programme (FP7/2007-2013) under grant agreement no. 270019 (SPACEBOOK project www.spacebook-project.org).

References

P. Bartie and W. Mackaness. 2013. D3.1.2: The SpaceBook City Model. Technical report, The SPACEBOOK Project (FP7/2011-2014 grant agreement no. 270019).

P. Bartie, W. Mackaness, M. Fredriksson, and J. Konigsmann. 2013. D2.1.2 Final Viewshed Component. Technical report, The SPACEBOOK Project (FP7/2011-2014 grant agreement no. 270019).

S. Janarthanam, O. Lemon, P. Bartie, T. Dalmas, A. Dickinson, X. Liu, W. Mackaness, and B. Webber. 2013. Evaluating a city exploration dialogue system combining question-answering and pedestrian navigation. In *Proc. ACL 2013*.

Oliver Lemon and Alexander Gruenstein. 2004. Multithreaded context for robust conversational interfaces: context-sensitive speech recognition and interpretation of corrective fragments. *ACM Transactions on Computer-Human Interaction (ACM TOCHI)*, 11(3):241– 267.

Oliver Lemon and Olivier Pietquin. 2007. Machine learning for spoken dialogue systems. In *Interspeech*.

Mikio Nakano, Kotaro Funakoshi, Yuji Hasegawa, and Hiroshi Tsujino. 2008. A framework for building conversational agents based on a multi-expert model. In *Proceedings of the 9th SIGdial Workshop on Discourse and Dialogue*, SIGdial '08, pages 88–91, Stroudsburg, PA, USA. Association for Computational Linguistics.

Fan Yang, Peter A. Heeman, and Andrew Kun. 2008. Switching to real-time tasks in multi-tasking dialogue. In *Proceedings of the 22Nd International Conference on Computational Linguistics - Volume 1*, COLING '08, pages 1025–1032, Stroudsburg, PA, USA. Association for Computational Linguistics.

Steve Young. 2000. Probabilistic methods in spoken dialogue systems. *Philosophical Transactions of the Royal Society (Series A)*, 358(1769):1389–1402.

Mostly Passive Information Delivery – a Prototype

J. Vystrčil, T. Macek, D. Luksch, M. Labský, L. Kunc, J. Kleindienst, T. Kašparová
IBM Prague Research and Development Lab
V Parku 2294/4, 148 00 Prague 4
Czech Republic
{jan_vystrcil, tomas_macek, david.luksch, martin_labsky, ladislav_kuncl, jankle, tereza.kasparova}@cz.ibm.com

Abstract

In this paper we introduce a new UI paradigm that mimics radio broadcast along with a prototype called Radio One. The approach aims to present useful information from multiple domains to mobile users (e.g. drivers on the go or cell phone users). The information is served in an entertaining manner in a mostly passive style – without the user having to ask for it– as in real radio broadcast. The content is generated on the fly by a machine and integrates a mix of personal (calendar, emails) and publicly available but customized information (news, weather, POIs). Most of the spoken audio output is machine synthesized. The implemented prototype permits passive listening as well as interaction using voice commands or buttons. Initial feedback gathered while testing the prototype while driving indicates good acceptance of the system and relatively low distraction levels.

1 Introduction

The main purpose of this paper is to describe a prototype of the Radio One concept. Radio One presents music, news, emails, relevant POI and other information to the user in a mostly passive way, similarly to conventional radios. Users can interract with the system as well using voice commands or buttons. The concept was refined and initially tested with prerecorded audio-visual scenarios using the Wizard-of-Oz (WOZ) technique (Macek et al., 2013).

Here we describe the early prototype implementation of the system and summarize initial feedback collected during informal testing.

2 Related Work

Applications that produce customized audio streams can be found in many online music delivery services including Spotify, Pandora, or iTunes. While the above services often focus on music only, other providers (BBC, CNN) publish their spoken content in the form of podcasts. Spoken audio used for podcasts is often recorded by professional speakers as opposed to the concept presented here. The Aha radio (Aha, 2014) provides various thematic streams of information including music, news, social network updates or Points of Interest (POI). Content can be selected manually by switching between channels. Similar strategies are utilized by Stitcher (Stitcher, 2014) and other services. The concept presented here attempts insted to preselect the content automatically and on the fly while preserving the option to request the content explicitely.

Many in-car infotainment systems adopted the use of voice control and utilize information directly from on-line services; e.g. (BMW, 2014) and (Ford, 2014). All of the abovementioned applications use mobile data connection to deliver audio stream (as opposed to text) to the user. This can lead to large data downloads and potentially to high bills from mobile network providers.

3 Radio One Concept

Radio One mimics radio broadcast by generating infotainment content on the fly. Unlike real radios, Radio One customizes its content to the particular listener and should even adapt automatically while the user interacts with it. In addition to the content typically played by radios, the synthetic content also includes private information like calendar or emails. Most of the spoken output is produced by a text-to-speech system with the exception of podcasts.

The presented information stream is sparse with

the intervals between spoken segments filled with music and moderator small-talk. The content structure is configurable and can be adapted both automatically, based on observing habits of the user, or via explicit voice commands or buttons.

The main benefit of dynamically generated content is that the system can easily include dynamic personal content and that the infotainment stream can be efficiently controlled by the user and influenced by the environment (such as expected duration of the drive or current road conditions). From a technical perspective, the connection requirements are much smaller compared to audio transfers, as Radio One mostly downloads textual feeds only. Downloading redundant information can be avoided by knowing what has already been presented to the particular user. Further, the user can navigate in the broadcast, either to specific topics by using voice commands, or just backward and forward by using buttons. This option should reduce potential stress related to a driver concentrating on a broadcasted topic knowing s/he would be unable to replay. The radio presents information from the covered domains continuously. The stream of presented information also serves as a natural way of teaching the user about the supported domains. By hearing that news are read as part of the radio stream, the user finds out that news is one category that can be requested by voice commands.

4 System Description

Although previous WOZ tests (Macek et al., 2013) were sufficient to collect the initial user feedback, their flexibility and fidelity was limited. The prototype described in this paper is intended for testing of concepts and for conducting realistic usability tests in a car. The implemented prototype is a fully functioning system, although still with a limited feature set.

4.1 Architecture

The overall architecture of the system is depicted in Figure 1. The system collects inputs both from manual controls (steering wheel buttons, rotary knob) and from ASR (voice commands). Multiple on-line and off-line data sources provide content. While driving, GPS information about the car position is used together with an optional calculated route and POI data to plan overall broadcasting. The core of the Radio One system (see

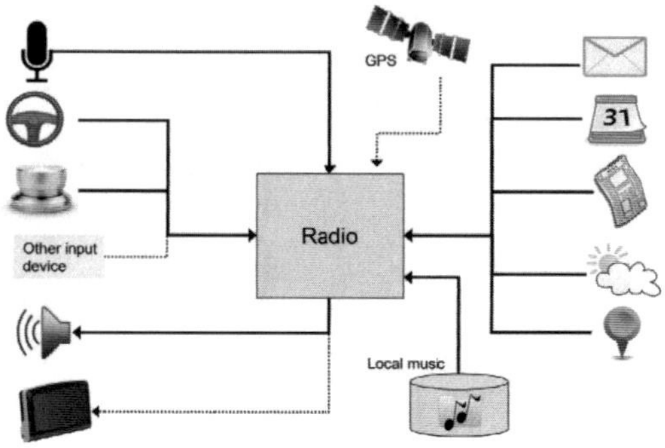

Figure 1: Radio One big picture.

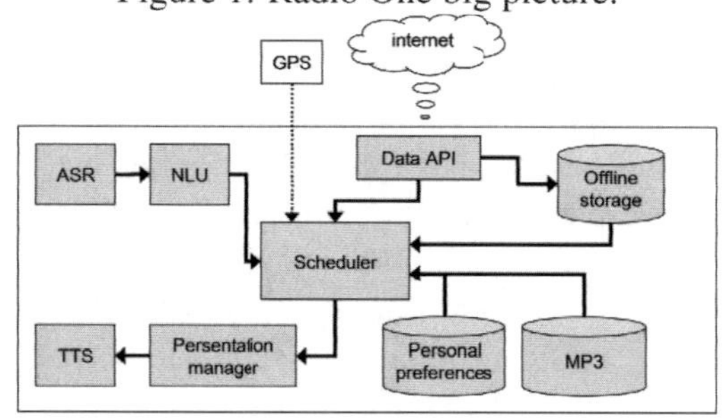

Figure 2: Radio One architecture.

Figure 2) is the scheduler. The scheduler is responsible for planning both the type of content and the time of its presentation. The content associated with higher expected cognitive load (e.g. emails or calendar) can be planned for segments of the journey that have low driving difficulty (e.g. straight highway). The overall architecture aims to be highly configurable and context-aware to be able to produce heterogeneous content based on differing user preferences and changing state of the environment.

4.2 Controls

Multiple *button* configurations are possible, ranging from a "speech button-only" setup to several buttons used to provide quick access to frequently used functions. For in-car setups, the availability of buttons is often limited. A configuration of 3 buttons in a row (in addition to speech button) can be used to let the user navigate back and forth using the two outer buttons and request more details or pause/resume the broadcast with a central button. Both "per-item" (e.g. single email, song or news title) and "per-bundle" navigation ("bundle" being a coherent group of affiliated items, e.g. emails) can be supported by short and long presses of the navigation buttons. Other functions would typically be available through voice commands only, or also through a touch interface where available (e.g. on a cell phone or in a parked car).

Alternatively to the buttons on the steering wheel, a *rotary knob* can be placed on the side of the driver's seat (depicted on the left of Figure 3). Usually, a single knob press initiates speech input, while turning the knob navigates back and forth in items. Per-bundle navigation can be triggered either by using greater turns or by turning the knob while pressed.

The voice control subsystem is hybrid with speech recognition and understanding being done both remotely and locally. This way, functions are available even when off-line while benefiting from improved accuracy and coverage of the server models when on-line. Free-form commands are understood (e.g. "email" or "would you read my email please").

4.3 Content and Presentation

Two *modes of operation* are implemented. The *off-line mode* permits testing with locally saved data or data specifically tailored for various experiments. The *on-line mode* collects data (e.g. email, calendar, news) periodically from the network and presents it at appropriate times.

News are collected periodically from configurable network sources and grouped by topic. Two forms of news presentation are implemented. A shorter version is used during news summaries. A longer version can be requested by an explicit voice request like "tell me more" or by pressing a "details" button.

Emails undergo elementary pre-processing to improve their suitability for being read out loud. Emails longer than a configured threshold are shortened at the end of the sentence. Email histories are also skipped. The user can request a full version of the email using a voice command like "read the whole message".

Moderator commentaries are tailored to the content they accompany. We use a set of handcrafted prompt templates for natural language generation. Prompt templates are grouped according to the context that triggers them into pools of alternatives, from which prompts are selected randomly while avoiding repetitions. Moderators can announce upcoming content or refer to content that just finished playing. Prompt templates often contain variables referring to various properties of the neighbouring content (e.g. name of the preceding song or topic of the upcoming news).

Information is presented as a story, typically with a brief summary-of-the-broadcast at the beginning. This order can be interrupted by sudden events (e.g. emails arriving, hot breaking news, POI announcements) with proper moderator comments to indicate what is happening. The information is grouped together in bundles of the same type (e.g. email summaries are not mixed with calendar or news items). Typical in-car presentation order starts with music to allow the listener to get concentrated on driving. Then a summary is provided followed by blocks of music and information bundles.

In contrast to our earlier WOZ study, the current version of the prototype does not present any visual information as we focus on the driving scenario. The previous WOZ study indicated that this information was distracting to the driver and not much valued by the participants.

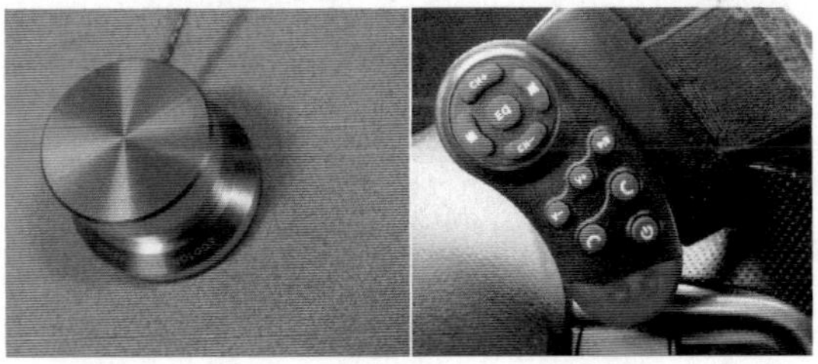

Figure 3: Alternative user interface controls

4.4 Implementation

The prototype is implemented in Java. It uses a local text-to-speech system (TTS). We use the Nuance Vocalizer premium voices to provide the best available TTS quality. Current implementation is primarily in English (moderators and their comments) although playback of content in other languages (currently Czech) is supported as well. Language detection is done automatically (Cybozu Labs, 2014). The system was tested both on a PC (Windows 7) and on tablets and phones (Android, Windows 8). Emails are currently retrieved using the IMAP protocol so various email providers can be used. News are currently downloaded from the Feedzilla (Feedzilla, 2014) REST API and from other RSS feeds.

Calendar events are retrieved from the user's Google Calendar account. The radio automatically announces individual upcoming events and also plays summaries about the remaining events of the day (also can be requested by voice).

Like real radios, we use characteristic earcons and jingles to introduce particular types of information (e.g. email, news or calendar) and other sounds to separate individual information items from each other (e.g. earcons between emails or news titles).

For testing purposes we use infra-red remote control buttons (see right hand part of Figure 3) mounted to the steering wheel, with key events received by a special purpose hardware and passed to Radio One via Bluetooth.

We use either an AUX cable or a radio FM transmitter to integrate with the car's audio system. The current prototype implements music playback, presents news, email, weather reports and calendar summaries. Initial work was done on presenting POIs near the current location. An arbitrary list of MP3 files can be used as a source of music. Ideally, user's own collection of music is used during the tests. ID3 tags of music files are utilized in the process of generating voice prompts spoken by moderators as part of their small talk (e.g. "This was a song by the Beatles").

5 Usability testing

Initially, a WOZ experiment was conducted without having the system implemented. Test subjects drove a low-fidelity driving simulator while listening to a radio stream broadcasted by the wizard, who played pre-recorded audio-visual snippets trying to satisfy user's requests. We described results of this experiment previously in (Macek et al., 2013). The main feedback from this experiment was that the users perceived the quality of synthesized speech sufficiently. The visual information shown by the wizard contained mostly static pictures or short texts in large fonts. Most of the users did not find the screen useful in this setup. Therefore the current radio prototype is screen-less. Two groups of users could be identified. The first one used the system in the same way as a standard radio, with minimal interaction. The other group preferred to be "in control" and used both buttons and voice commands to ask for specific content.

Multiple informal tests were conducted by 4 test drivers in real traffic. More extensive testing is still in preparation. The feedback collected so far was positive, indicating that the TTS quality was sufficient. Even with a small number of test drivers it became apparent that the roles of customization and automatic adaptation to preferences of a specific user will be crucial.

Information-heavy content like certain kinds of news was sometimes considered difficult to listen to while driving, which was in part due to all of the test drivers being non-native speakers of English. Adding jingles to separate the presented news items from one another improved the perception of the system significantly. The news feeds used by the prototype were originally not intended for audio presentation, which does impact their understandability, but the effect does not seem to be major. Lighter content like weather forecasts and calendar announcements were considered easy to understand.

The test drivers considered it important to be able to use their personal data (news, email, music). This motivated the inclusion of information sources in languages other than English and the addition of automatic language identification so as to select proper TTS voices. The fact that multiple languages were present in the broadcast was not perceived adversely. One shortcoming of the tested system was still a low variability of moderators' comments.

6 Conclusion

We presented a work-in-progress demonstration prototype of a novel method for presenting information to users on-the-go. A preceding WOZ study indicated promising user acceptance which was also confirmed using the described prototype. When comparing with existing systems, the system presented here has much lower requirements on communication bandwidth, requires less human work for content authoring and permits a higher level of personalization. Amount of interactivity depends very much on user preferences.

In future work we would like to pay attention to evaluation of user feedback on more extensive usability tests. It will be interesting to see to what extent the user will opt for active interaction with the system and for the particular interaction techniques.

Acknowledgments

The presented work is part of an IBM and Nuance joint research project.

References

Harman International Aha. 2014. Aha radio website. Retrieved from http://www.aharadio.com/.

BMW. 2014. Bmw connecteddrive services. Retrieved from http://www.bmw.com/com/en/insights/technology/connecteddrive/2013/services_apps/bmw_connecteddrive_services.html.

Inc. Cybozu Labs. 2014. Language detection library for java. Retrieved from https://code.google.com/p/language-detection/.

Feedzilla. 2014. Feedzilla - news feed directory. Retrieved from http://www.feedzilla.com/.

Ford. 2014. Sync with myford touch. Retrieved from http://www.ford.com/technology/sync/.

Tomáš Macek, Tereza Kašparová, Jan Kleindienst, Ladislav Kunc, Martin Labský, and Jan Vystrčil. 2013. Mostly passive information delivery in a car. In *Proceedings of the 5th International Conference on Automotive User Interfaces and Interactive Vehicular Applications*, AutomotiveUI '13, pages 250–253, New York, NY, USA. ACM.

Inc. Stitcher. 2014. Stitcher website. Retrieved from http://www.stitcher.com/.

Navigation Dialog of Blind People: Recovery from Getting Lost

Jan Vystrcil, Ivo Maly, Jan Balata and Zdenek Mikovec
Czech Technical University in Prague, Faculty Of Electrical Engineering
Karlovo nam. 13, 121 35 Praha 2
Czech Republic
{vystrjan, malyil, balatjan, xmikovec}@fel.cvut.cz

Abstract

Navigation of blind people is different from the navigation of sighted people and there is also difference when the blind person is recovering from getting lost. In this paper we focus on qualitative analysis of dialogs between lost blind person and navigator, which is done through the mobile phone. The research was done in two outdoor and one indoor location. The analysis revealed several areas where the dialog model must focus on detailed information, like evaluation of instructions provided by blind person and his/her ability to reliably locate navigation points.

1 Introduction

When blind people travel independently, it may happen that they get lost. This happens when they can not find any useful navigation points. Use of existing GPS based navigation systems is of no use as the maps do not provide appropriate navigation points and the GPS localization is imprecise (tens of meters, where the lost blind person needs precision at highest in meters). In such situation blind people typically use one of two following methods to recover. First they can ask people in their surrounding for help. Second they can call friend or dedicated assistance center. The first method is currently more favorable for blind people, but they have experience with both methods. In each method the dialog has different structure due to the different context information available to the helping person (called navigator) and lost blind person.

In our research we focus on the second method, navigation through mobile phone call. Balata et al. (2013b) showed that such method is usable and navigator can successfully guide blind person in outdoor environment. This is because the blind person is able to efficiently describe his/her position. Balata et al. (2013a) found that there is quite good coverage of locations that are very well known to blind persons and that they should be able to navigate other lost blind person there.

These findings show that building some kind of assistance center where blind people can help each other is a promising idea. Our intention is to extend such a center in a way that the helping person will be replaced by natural language based dialog system. According to Pittermann (2005) this dialog system belongs to the category "Dialog as purposeful activity" with overlapping to the category "Dialogue as collaborative activity". The key questions we focus on are:

- How the selection of an appropriate form of language depends on aspects of the environment?
- What is the structure of the dialog with respect to the environment?

In the initial step of this work-in-progress research, we want to analyze the communication between lost blind person and the navigator in order to analyze the dialog structure and make initial observation about the context information interchange and verification dialog. Such dialog is very important for navigator to find out, where exactly the blind person get lost. With the knowledge of the way of communication between lost blind person and navigator we will be able in the future replace the navigator with a navigation system based on natural language understanding.

In order to gather and analyze initial data we ran an experiment in which the blind person got lost and was asked to call the assistance center which mediated connection to suitable navigator. Together, they tried to find the actual position of blind person and they tried to navigate him/her to end of the track.

2 Related Work

Many current dialog systems are based on statistical approach when analyzing the semantics of spoken dialog as presented by Jurcicek (2007). Using belief state tracking provides better results for cases of noisy input. Ma et al. (2012) introduced system that is combining geographical knowledge of landmarks with dialog system itself and work with probabilities of particular locations.

Recovering from lost scenario can be also compared to robot localization problem as presented by Thrun (1998) and Thrun et al. (2001), more exactly to kidnapped robot problem, where robot with knowledge of its position is moved to different location without providing this information to the robot. This scenario is testing the ability of robot to recover from being lost while expecting to be on another place. These methods are based on probabilistic algorithms, working with probabilities of measurement while being on a certain place.

However we do not expect blind person to wear any precise sensors for distance measurements and localization, we can benefit from his/her senses (touch, hearing and olfaction) that can provide set of reliable observations.

3 Experiment Description

3.1 Collected Data

We set up an experiment in order to collect and analyze initial data about the dialog structure of lost blind person and sighted navigator person. During the experiment we recorded the course of the test with two cameras, one was on the blind person's shoulder and one was used for 3rd person view of the scene in order to show context (environment) of the test. Moreover, we recorded the blind person's position using GPS coordinates in outdoor and blind person's interaction with mobile navigation application. Camera recordings and GPS logs were used only for post-test evaluation. The dialog between the blind person and navigator was recorded and annotated.

3.2 Participants

For the experiment, 13 blind people, 8 female and 5 male, were invited by e-mail and following snowball effect. All the participants had blindness of category 4 and 5 – according to ICD-10 WHO classification.

3.3 Procedure

In the experiment, we focused on three types of location, two outdoor and one indoor: city center streets (track A), open city park (track B) and university building (track C). We selected these three types of location in order to analyze possible differences in the dialog structure or types of provided information.

The script of the experiment was similar for each type of location. The participant was given a mobile phone with mobile navigation application for blind called NaviTerier Vystrcil et al. (2012). NaviTerier provides TTS synthesized description of the predefined track divided into segments. For each segment the description of the environment and navigation to the next segment was tailored with respect to the way how blind people navigate. Borders of segments are selected on places that could be easily recognizable by blind people (e.g. corner of building, doors, etc.). Each participant had a goal to go from start point to the end of the track using the mobile navigation application for blind. In order to put the participant into the "recovery from lost" situation, the navigation instructions were intentionally modified to represent a mistake in the track description (a realistic mistake), which caused that the participant get lost. When the participant realized that he/she is lost, a navigator from assistance center was called and they tried to find out the location of blind person and navigate him/her to the end of the track.

Navigator was seated in an office without visual contact to lost blind person. He knew all three routes very well. The only source of information about the lost blind person was dialog done by a phone call.

3.3.1 Track A - City Center Streets

In track A the participant was asked to navigate to the Vaclavska passage, see Figure 1. The navigation instruction were changed so that the two streets (Trojanova and Jenstejnska) were switched so that the participant get lost at the T crossing of Jenstejnska and Vaclavska street. The navigation using the mobile navigation application for blind in this type of environment was easy for participants and they all get lost at the desired location.

The navigator and participant had several navigation points there to get oriented. First of all, there was a nearby busy street Resslova, which can be heard. Next there was a closed gateway with metal gate, which is quite unique for this location. There were also waste bins (containers), phone booth and entrance to the underground garage.

3.3.2 Track B - Open City Park

In track B the participant was asked to navigate through the park to the restaurant, see Figure 1. The navigation instruction were changed so that the two junctions were skipped and the participant ended near the middle of the park, where fountain is located.

In this type of location, there were also not many unique navigation points. The most usable were two perpendicular streets with trams, the fountain in the middle of the park and two unique stairs. There were also multiple benches and grass plots.

3.3.3 Track C - Building

In track C the participant was asked to navigate through the building from the entrance to the yard, see Figure 1. The navigation instructions were changed so that instead of taking stairs down, the participant was asked to take stairs up and he/she got lost in the small corridor, where the last doors should be located but they were not there. The navigation using the NaviTerier application in this type of environment was easy for the participants and they all get lost at the desired location.

At the place, where the participant got lost, there were several navigation points. First point was showcase from metal and glass at the expected location of doors to the yard. Then there was wooden door secured with metal bars and wooden stairs going up and down.

Figure 1: Visualization of individual tracks A, B and C used in the experiment. The intended path is shown by solid line. Path shown by dashed line shows the real path leading to the point, where the participant got lost – yellow exclamation mark – and from where the participant was navigated back to the path.

4 Results and Discussion

In the track A and track C, the participants got lost at location very well known to the navigator, thus the identification of lost blind person location was mostly fast and easy. In the track B, participants got sometimes lost at locations unfamiliar for the navigator due to the ambiguity of the environment and thus the location identification process was complicated.

The dialog structure of the communication between lost blind person and the navigator corresponds to the model introduced by Balata et al. (2013b). At the beginning the blind person describes his/her location, track instructions and the problem description, i.e. what is the difference between instructions of navigation application and reality. After the beginning the dialog continues by iterative searching of unique navigation points that may help the navigator to find the position and orientation of the lost blind person, until he/she gets to the location from which he/she can continue with the track. The dialog system should take into account following findings about the dialog structure.

When the blind person get lost, he/she uses information, provided by navigation application for sections that seemed to him/her correct and corresponding with reality, for description of his/her current position, e.g. "I am in the Vaclavska street." The dialog system should take into account uncertainty of information provided by lost blind person, possibility that the blind person got lost much earlier and the navigation instructions for next several segments were corresponding with the reality by coincidence.

The fact that the blind person gets lost is little bit stressy for him/her. Therefor he/she may provide illogical answers to some questions, e.g.

Q: "Could you provide me with the description of your current position?" and A: "I would rather go to the start of the track and describe the track from the beginning."

Description of current position of blind person is very different from the description of sighted person. The dialog system should take into account that the blind person may not find particular navigation point, but it does not mean that the navigation point is not there. Moreover, some navigation points may be difficult or impossible to find by blind person. Similar issue is identification of particular navigation points. The blind person may have difficulties to distinguish between bend, turning, intersection and end of pavement. This may be misleading to dialog system. On the other hand, when the blind person confirms that particular navigation point was found, the system should check, if it is really the one, e.g. when doors are found, the system should check the material or type of the doors.

Blind persons use other senses than sight to scan the current position and navigation points. Even though the senses are more sensitive, the provided information may not be accurate, e.g. the blind person is reporting inclining pavement and in reality there is flat pavement.

It seems that the preferred sense is connected with the type of environment. In the track B with low density of navigation points which are ambiguous the blind persons preferred hearing.

Some navigation points are not permanent and may by varying. E.g. when there are two streets, one near (not busy) and one far (busy) and the blind person is asked to locate busy street, this information will depend on the current traffic on both streets. Together with the fact that term busy is subjective, the blind person may locate wrong street.

Some blind persons (the ones with high confidence of independency and orientation skills) tended to get oriented independently to the dialog with navigator. That means they provided the navigator with required information, but at the same time they were moving and they were disrupting the navigators mental model of the blind person's location.

There is not a standardized vocabulary how blind persons describe objects. Therefore they tend to use wide range of words and also metaphoric descriptions to describe the same object.

5 Conclusion and Future Work

In this paper, we did initial analysis of dialogs between blind person, who got lost when walking on a track with the instructions from mobile navigation application, and navigator, who is trying to help him get oriented. The research was done in three different locations, in city center streets, in open city park and in building. The dialog between blind person and navigator was recorded and qualitatively analyzed in order to reveal dialog features which can be used for improvement of the navigation itself and later it can help to replace the human navigator with automated system.

Initial analysis showed that the type of location may have impact on strategy, how the blind person explore his/her surroundings and how he/she tries to get oriented. In city center streets (track A) and in building (track C) the blind persons were able to explore their surroundings and they allowed the navigator to find out, where they probably are. In open city park (track B) the blind persons had problem to find navigation points and sometimes they were trying to get oriented independently, which led to the difficulties for navigator to find their position. In many cases, the blind persons were using the information from mobile navigation application until the point where they got lost. Unfortunately, such information may already be misleading. As a general finding, the dialog should focus also on verification of navigation points, which may not be permanent (e.g. finding busy street, when there are more streets around) or which may be not identified in not enough detail.

In future, we would like to focus on individual aspects found in qualitative analysis and design strategies into the dialog model between lost blind person and navigator and evaluate it quantitatively.

Acknowledgments

This research has been supported by the project Design of special user interfaces funded by grant no. SGS13/213/OHK3/3T/13 (FIS 161 – 832130C000).

References

J. Balata, J. Franc, Z. Mikovec, and P. Slavik. 2013a. Collaborative navigation of visually impaired. *Journal on Multimodal User Interfaces*, pages 1–11.

J. Balata, Z. Mikovec, and J. Novacek. 2013b. Field study: How Blind People Communicate While Recovering From Loss of Orientation. In *Cognitive Infocommunications (CogInfoCom), 2013 IEEE 4th International Conference on*, pages 313–317, Budapest. IEEE Hungary Section, University Obuda.

Filip Jurcicek. 2007. Statistical approach to the semantic analysis of spoken dialogues.

Yi Ma, Antoine Raux, Deepak Ramachandran, and Rakesh Gupta. 2012. Landmark-based location belief tracking in a spoken dialog system. In *Proceedings of the 13th Annual Meeting of the Special Interest Group on Discourse and Dialogue*, SIGDIAL '12, pages 169–178, Stroudsburg, PA, USA. Association for Computational Linguistics.

Johannes Pittermann. 2005. Spoken dialogue technology: Toward the conversational user interface by michael f. mctear. *Comput. Linguist.*, 31(3):403–406, September.

Sebastian Thrun, Dieter Fox, Wolfram Burgard, and Frank Dellaert. 2001. Robust monte carlo localization for mobile robots. *Artificial Intelligence*, 128(12):99 – 141.

Sebastian Thrun. 1998. Bayesian landmark learning for mobile robot localization. *Machine Learning*, 33(1):41–76.

J. Vystrcil, Z. Mikovec, and P. Slavik. 2012. Naviterier – indoor navigation system for visually impaired. In *SMART HOMES 2012*, pages 25–28. Czech Technical University.

Conversational Strategies for Robustly Managing Dialog in Public Spaces

Aasish Pappu **Ming Sun** **Seshadri Sridharan** **Alexander I. Rudnicky**
Language Technologies Institute
Carnegie Mellon University
Pittsburgh PA, USA
{aasish,mings,seshadrs,air}@cs.cmu.edu

Abstract

Open environments present an attention management challenge for conversational systems. We describe a kiosk system (based on Ravenclaw–Olympus) that uses simple auditory and visual information to interpret human presence and manage the system's attention. The system robustly differentiates intended interactions from unintended ones at an accuracy of 93% and provides similar task completion rates in both a quiet room and a public space.

1 Introduction

Dialog systems designers try to minimize disruptive influences by introducing physical and behavioral constraints to create predictable environments. This includes using a closed-talking microphone or limiting interaction to one user at a time. But such constraints are difficult to apply in public environments such as kiosks (Bohus and Horvitz, 2010; Foster et al., 2012; Nakashima et al., 2014), in-car assistants (Kun et al., 2007; Hofmann et al., 2013; Misu et al., 2013) or on mobile robots (Haasch et al., 2004; Sabanovic et al., 2006; Kollar et al., 2012). To implement dialog systems that operate in public spaces, we have to relax some of these constraints and deal with additional challenges. For example, the system needs to select the correct interlocutor, who may be only one of several possible ones in the vicinity, then determine whether they are initiating the process of engaging with the system.

In this paper we focus on the problems of identifying a potential interlocutor in the environment, engaging them in conversation and providing suitable channel-maintenance cues (Bruce et al., 2002; Fukuda et al., 2002; Al Moubayed and Skantze, 2011). We address these problems in the context of a simple application, a kiosk agent that accepts tasks such as taking a message to a named recipient. To evaluate the effectiveness of our approach we compared the system's ability to manage conversations in a quiet room and in a public area.

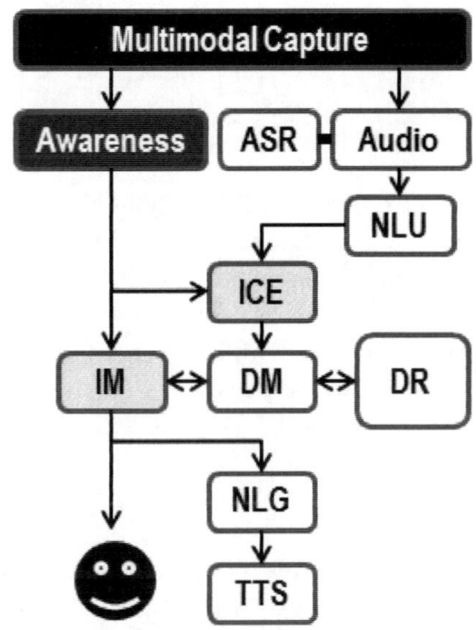

Figure 1: Ravenclaw–Olympus augmented with multimodal input and output functions.

The remainder of this paper is organized as follows: we first describe the system architecture, then present the evaluation setup and the results, then review related work and finally conclude with an analysis of the study.

2 System Architecture

Figure 1 shows the architecture; it incorporates Ravenclaw/Olympus (Bohus et al., 2007) standard components (in white), new components (in black) and modified ones (shaded). In the system pipeline, the Audio Server receives audio from a microphone, endpoints it and sends it to the ASR

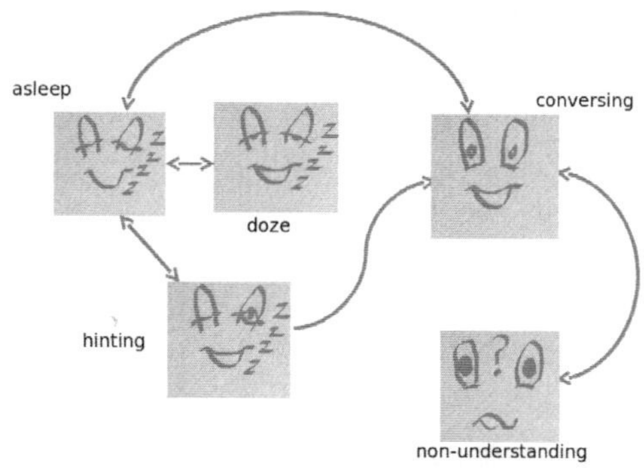

Figure 2: Face states; some are animations.

engine (PocketSphinx); the decoding is passed to NLU (Phoenix parser). ICE (Input Confidence Estimation) (Helios) assigns confidence scores for the input concepts. Based on user's input and the context, the Dialog Manager (DM) determines what to do next, perhaps using data from the Domain Reasoner (DR). An Interaction Manager (IM) initiates a spoken response using Natural Language Generation (NLG) and Text-to-Speech (TTS) component.

Three components were added: (1) *Multimodal Capture* acquires audio and human position data using a Kinect device [1]. (2) *Awareness* determines whether there is a potential interlocutor in the vicinity and their current position, using skeletal and azimuth information. (3) *Talking Head* that conveys the system's state (as shown in Figure 2): whether it's active (*conversing* and *hinting*) or idle (*asleep* and *doze*) and whether focused concepts are grounded (*conversing* and *non-understanding*); certain state representations (e.g., *conversing*) are coordinated with the TTS component.

3 Evaluation

A robust system should be able to function as well in a difficult situation as in a controlled one. We compare the system's performance in two environments, public and quiet, and evaluate the (a) system's awareness of intended users, and its (b) end-to-end performance.

The same twenty subjects participated in both experiments: a mix of American, Indian, Chinese and Hispanic with different fluency levels of English. None of them had previously interacted with this system prior to this study.

The subjects were told that they would interact with a virtual agent displayed on a screen. Their task for the awareness experiment was to make the agent aware that they wished to interact. For the end-to-end system performance, the task was to instruct the agent to send a message to a named recipient.

3.1 Situated Awareness

We define situated awareness as correctly engaging the intended interlocutor (i.e., verbally acknowledge the user's presence) under two conditions. When the user is positioned (i) inside the visual range of the Kinect at LOC-0 in Figure 3(a); and (ii) outside the visual range of the Kinect at LOC-1 in Figure 3(a). We used the effective range of the camera's documented horizontal field of view (57°); hereafter referred as its *cone-of-awareness*.

We conducted the awareness experiment in a public space, a lounge at a hub connecting multiple corridors. The area has tables and seating, self-serve coffee, a microwave oven, etc. The experiment was conducted during regular hours, between 10am to 6pm on weekdays. During these times we observed occupants discussing projects, preparing food, making coffee, etc. No direct attempt was made to influence their behavior and we believe that they made no attempt to accommodate our activities. Accordingly, the natural sound level in the room varied in unpredictable ways. To supplement naturally-occurring sounds, we played audio of a conversation between two humans, an extract from the SwitchBoard corpus (Graff et al., 2001). It was played using a loudspeaker placed at LOC-2 in Figure 3(a). The locations (0, 1, and 2) are all 1.5m from the Kinect, which we deemed to be a comfortable distance for the subjects. LOC-1 and LOC-2 are 70° to the left and right of the Kinect, outside its cone.

To detect the presence of an intended user, we build an awareness model that uses three sensory streams viz., voice activity, skeleton, and sound source azimuth. This model relies on the coincidence of azimuth angle and the skeleton angle (along with voice activity) to determine the presence of an intended user. We compare the pro-

[1] See `http://www.microsoft.com/en-us/Kinectforwindows/develop/`. Three sources are tapped: the beam-formed audio, the sound source azimuth and skeleton coordinates. Video data are not used.

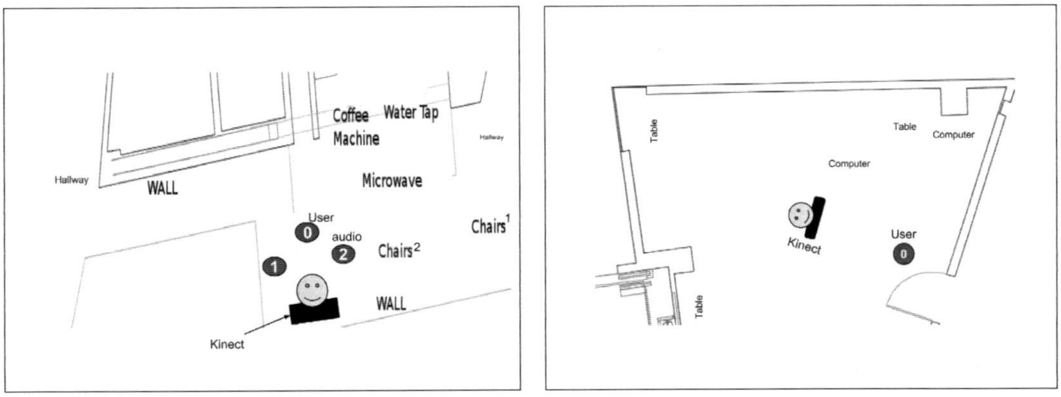

Figure 3: (a) Plan of Public Space (lounge);(b) Plan of Quiet Room (lab). Dark circled markers indicate locations (LOC-0, LOC-1, LOC-2), discussed in the text.

Condition	Voice	+Skeleton	+Azimuth
Outside the cone	28%	–	**93%**
Inside the cone	–	25%	**93%**

Table 1: Accuracy for the Awareness Detection

posed model with two baselines: (1) conventional voice-activity-detection (VAD): once speech is detected the system responds as if a conversation is initiated and (2) based on skeleton plus VAD: once the skeleton appears in front of the Kinect and a voice is heard, the system engages in conversation.

Table 1 shows the combination of sensory streams we used under two conditions. For the outside-the-cone condition, the participants stand in LOC-1 as shown in Figure 3(a) and follow the instructions from the agent. Initially, the subject's skeleton is invisible to the agent; however the subject is audible to the agent. Therefore, in certain combinations of sensors (e.g., `voice + skeleton` model and `voice + skeleton + azimuth` model) the system attempts to guide them to move in front of it, i.e. to LOC-0, an ideal position for interacting with the system. For inside-the-cone condition, subjects stand at LOC-0 where the agent can sense their skeleton.

When user stands at LOC-1 i.e., outside-the-cone `voice + skeleton model` and `voice + skeleton + azimuth` models are functionally the same since the source of distraction has no skeleton in the cone. When user stands at LOC-0, i.e., inside-the-cone `voice` alone is the same as `voice + skeleton` model since the agent always sees a skeleton in front of it. Therefore, this variant was not used.

We treated awareness detection as a binary decision. An utterance is classified either as "intended" or "unintended". We manually labeled the utterances whether they were directed at the system ("intended"), "unintended" otherwise. Accuracy on "intended" speech is reported in the Table 1. Within each condition, the order of the experiments with different awareness strategies was randomized.

We observe that the `voice + skeleton + azimuth` model proves to be robust in the public space. Its performance is significantly better, $t(38) = 8.1$, $p \approx 0.001$, compared to the other baselines in both conditions. This result agrees with previous research (Haasch et al., 2004; Bohus and Horvitz, 2009) showing that a fusion of multimodal features improves performance over a unimodal approach. Our result indicates that a simple heuristic approach, using minimal visual and audio features, provides usable attention management in open environments. This approach helped the system handle a complex interaction scenario such as out-of-cone speech directed to the system. If the speaker is out of range but is producing possibly system-directed utterances, system urges them to step to the front. We believe it can be extended to other complex cases by introducing additional logic.

3.2 End-to-End System Performance

To investigate the effect of the environment, we compare the system's performance in public space and quiet room. The average noise level in the quiet room is about 47dB(A) with computers as

Metric	Public Space	Quiet Room
Success Ratio	15/20	16/20
Avg # Turns	14.2	16.4
Concept Acc	67%	68%

Table 2: Public Space vs Quiet Room Performance

the primary source of noise. The background sound level in the public space was 46dB; other natural sources ranged up to 57dB. The audio distractor measured 57dB. The same ASR acoustic models and processing parameters were used in both environments. The participant stood at LOC-0 in Figure 3(a) during the public space experiment and Figure 3(b) during the quiet room experiment. In both experiments, LOC-0 is 1.5m away from the system. We used the `voice + skeleton + azimuth` model to discriminate user speech from distractions in the environment.

We gave each participant a randomized series of message-sending tasks, e.g. "send a message to ⟨person⟩ who is in room ⟨number⟩". Subjects had a maximum of 3 minutes to complete; each task required 7 turns. The number of tasks completed (over the group) is reported in terms of task "success-ratio". Table 2 shows the success-ratio of the task, the average number of turns needed to complete the task, and the system's per-utterance concept accuracy (Boros et al., 1996). There were no statistically significant differences between quiet room and public space, ($t(38) < 2, p > 0.5$, on any metric). We conclude that the channel maintenance technique we tested was equally effective in both environments.

4 Related Work

The problem of deploying social agents in public spaces has been of enduring interest; (Bohus and Horvitz, 2010) list engagement as a challenge for a physically situated agent in open-world interactions. But the problem was noted earlier and solutions were proposed; e.g a "push-to-talk" protocol to signal the onset of intended user speech (Stent et al., 1999). (Sharp et al., 1997; Hieronymus et al., 2006) described the use of attention phrase as a required prefix to each user input. Although explicit actions are effective, they need to be learned by users. This may not be practical for systems in public areas engaged by casual users.

A more robust approach involves fusing several sources of information such as audio, gaze and pose(Horvitz et al., 2003; Bohus and Horvitz, 2009) (Hosoya et al., 2009; Nakano and Ishii, 2010). Previous works have shown that fusion of different sensory information can improve attention management. The drawback of such approaches is in the complexity of the sensor equipment. Our work attempts to create the relevant capabilities using a simple sensing device and relying on explicitly modeled conversational strategies. Others are also using the Microsoft Kinect device for research in dialog. For example, (Skantze and Al Moubayed, 2012) and (Foster et al., 2012) presented a multiparty interaction systems that use Kinect for face tracking and skeleton tracking combined with speech recognition.

In our current work, we show that situational awareness can be integrated into an existing dialog framework, Ravenclaw–Olympus, that was not originally designed with this functionality in mind. The source code of the framework presented in this work is publicly available for download [1] and the acoustic models that have been adapted to the Kinect audio channel [2]

5 Conclusion

We found that a conventional spoken dialog system can be adapted to a public space with minimal modifications to accommodate additional information sources. Investigating the effectiveness of different awareness strategies, we found that a simple heuristic approach that uses a combination of sensory streams viz., voice, skeleton and azimuth, can reliably identify the likely interlocutor. End-to-end system performance in a public space is similar to that observed in a quiet room, indicating that, at least under the conditions we created, usable performance can be achieved. This is a useful finding. We believe that on this level, channel maintenance is a matter of articulating a model that specifies appropriate behavior in different states defined by a small number of discrete features (presence, absence, coincidence). We conjecture that such a framework is likely to be extensible to more complex situations, for example ones involving multiple humans in the environment.

[1] http://trac.speech.cs.cmu.edu/repos/olympus/tags/KinectOly2.0/

[2] http://trac.speech.cs.cmu.edu/repos/olympus/tags/KinectOly2.0/Resources/DecoderConfig/AcousticModels/Semi_Kinect.cd_semi_5000/

References

[Al Moubayed and Skantze2011] S. Al Moubayed and G. Skantze. 2011. Turn-taking control using gaze in multiparty human-computer dialogue: Effects of 2d and 3d displays. In *Proceedings of AVSP, Florence, Italy*, pages 99–102.

[Bohus and Horvitz2009] D. Bohus and E. Horvitz. 2009. Dialog in the open world: platform and applications. In *Proceedings of the 2009 international conference on Multimodal interfaces*, pages 31–38. ACM.

[Bohus and Horvitz2010] D. Bohus and E. Horvitz. 2010. On the challenges and opportunities of physically situated dialog. In *2010 AAAI Fall Symposium on Dialog with Robots*. AAAI.

[Bohus et al.2007] D. Bohus, A. Raux, T.K. Harris, M. Eskenazi, and A.I. Rudnicky. 2007. Olympus: an open-source framework for conversational spoken language interface research. In *Proceedings of the workshop on bridging the gap: Academic and industrial research in dialog technologies*, pages 32–39. Association for Computational Linguistics.

[Boros et al.1996] M. Boros, W. Eckert, F. Gallwitz, G. Gorz, G. Hanrieder, and H. Niemann. 1996. Towards understanding spontaneous speech: Word accuracy vs. concept accuracy. In *Spoken Language, 1996. ICSLP 96. Proceedings., Fourth International Conference on*, volume 2, pages 1009–1012. IEEE.

[Bruce et al.2002] A. Bruce, I. Nourbakhsh, and R. Simmons. 2002. The role of expressiveness and attention in human-robot interaction. In *Proceedings of 2002 IEEE International Conference on Robotics and Automation*, volume 4, pages 4138–4142. IEEE.

[Foster et al.2012] M.E. Foster, A. Gaschler, M. Giuliani, A. Isard, M. Pateraki, and R.P.A. Petrick. 2012. "two people walk into a bar": Dynamic multi-party social interaction with a robot agent. In *Proc. of the 14th ACM International Conference on Multimodal Interaction ICMI.*

[Fukuda et al.2002] T. Fukuda, J. Taguri, F. Arai, M. Nakashima, D. Tachibana, and Y. Hasegawa. 2002. Facial expression of robot face for human-robot mutual communication. In *Proceedings of 2002 IEEE International Conference on Robotics and Automation*, volume 1, pages 46–51. IEEE.

[Graff et al.2001] D. Graff, K. Walker, and D. Miller. 2001. Switchboard cellular part 1 transcribed audio. In *Linguistic Data Consortium, Philadelphia.*

[Haasch et al.2004] A. Haasch, S. Hohenner, S. Hüwel, M. Kleinehagenbrock, S. Lang, I. Toptsis, GA Fink, J. Fritsch, B. Wrede, and G. Sagerer. 2004. Biron–the bielefeld robot companion. In *Proc. Int. Workshop on Advances in Service Robotics*, pages 27–32. Stuttgart, Germany: Fraunhofer IRB Verlag.

[Hieronymus et al.2006] J. Hieronymus, G. Aist, and J. Dowding. 2006. Open microphone speech understanding: correct discrimination of in domain speech. In *Proceedings of 2006 IEEE international conference on acoustics, speech, and signal processing*, volume 1. IEEE.

[Hofmann et al.2013] H. Hofmann, U. Ehrlich, A. Berton, A. Mahr, R. Math, and C. Müller. 2013. Evaluation of speech dialog strategies for internet applications in the car. In *Proceedings of the SIGDIAL 2013 Conference*, pages 233–241, Metz, France, August. Association for Computational Linguistics.

[Horvitz et al.2003] E. Horvitz, C. Kadie, T. Paek, and D. Hovel. 2003. Models of attention in computing and communication: from principles to application. In *Communications of the ACM*, volume 46, pages 52–59.

[Hosoya et al.2009] K. Hosoya, T. Ogawa, and T. Kobayashi. 2009. Robot auditory system using head-mounted square microphone array. In *Intelligent Robots and Systems, 2009. IROS 2009. IEEE/RSJ International Conference on*, pages 2736–2741. IEEE.

[Kollar et al.2012] T. Kollar, A. Vedantham, C. Sobel, C. Chang, V. Perera, and M. Veloso. 2012. A multi-modal approach for natural human-robot interaction. In *Proceedings of 2012 International Conference on Social Robots.*

[Kun et al.2007] A. Kun, T. Paek, and Z. Medenica. 2007. The effect of speech interface accuracy on driving performance. In *INTERSPEECH*, pages 1326–1329.

[Misu et al.2013] T. Misu, A. Raux, I. Lane, J. Devassy, and R. Gupta. 2013. Situated multi-modal dialog system in vehicles. In *Proceedings of the 6th Workshop on Eye Gaze in Intelligent Human Machine Interaction: Gaze in Multimodal Interaction*, pages 25–28. ACM.

[Nakano and Ishii2010] Y. Nakano and R. Ishii. 2010. Estimating user's engagement from eye-gaze behaviors in human-agent conversations. In *Proceedings of the 15th international conference on Intelligent user interfaces*, pages 139–148. ACM.

[Nakashima et al.2014] Taichi Nakashima, Kazunori Komatani, and Satoshi Sato. 2014. Integration of multiple sound source localization results for speaker identification in multiparty dialogue system. In *Natural Interaction with Robots, Knowbots and Smartphones*, pages 153–165. Springer New York.

[Sabanovic et al.2006] S. Sabanovic, M.P. Michalowski, and R. Simmons. 2006. Robots in the wild: Observing human-robot social interaction outside the lab. In *Advanced Motion Control, 2006. 9th IEEE International Workshop on*, pages 596–601. IEEE.

[Sharp et al.1997] R.D. Sharp, E. Bocchieri, C. Castillo, S. Parthasarathy, C. Rath, M. Riley, and J. Rowland. 1997. The watson speech recognition engine. In *Proceedings of 1997 IEEE international conference on acoustics, speech, and signal processing*, volume 5, pages 4065–4068. IEEE.

[Skantze and Al Moubayed2012] G. Skantze and S. Al Moubayed. 2012. Iristk: a statechart-based toolkit for multi-party face-to-face interaction. In *Proc. of the 14th ACM International Conference on Multimodal Interaction ICMI.*

[Stent et al.1999] A. Stent, J. Dowding, J. Gawron, E. Bratt, and R. Moore. 1999. The commandtalk spoken dialogue system. In *Proceedings of the 37th annual meeting of the Association for Computational Linguistics on Computational Linguistics*, pages 183–190. ACL.

Situationally Aware In-Car Information Presentation Using Incremental Speech Generation: Safer, and More Effective

Spyros Kousidis[1], **Casey Kennington**[1,2], **Timo Baumann**[4], **Hendrik Buschmeier**[2,3], **Stefan Kopp**[2,3], and **David Schlangen**[1]
[1]Dialogue Systems Group, [2]CITEC, [3]Sociable Agents Group – Bielefeld University
[4]Department of Informatics, Natural Language Systems Division – University of Hamburg
spyros.kousidis@uni-bielefeld.de

Abstract

Holding non-co-located conversations while driving is dangerous (Horrey and Wickens, 2006; Strayer et al., 2006), much more so than conversations with physically present, "situated" interlocutors (Drews et al., 2004). In-car dialogue systems typically resemble non-co-located conversations more, and share their negative impact (Strayer et al., 2013). We implemented and tested a simple strategy for making in-car dialogue systems aware of the driving situation, by giving them the capability to interrupt themselves when a dangerous situation is detected, and resume when over. We show that this improves both driving performance and recall of system-presented information, compared to a non-adaptive strategy.

1 Introduction

Imagine you are driving on a relatively free highway at a constant speed and you are talking with the person next to you. Suddenly, you need to overtake another car. This requires more attention from you; you check the mirrors before you change lanes, and again before you change back. Plausibly, an attentive passenger would have noticed your attention being focused more on the driving, and reacted to this by interrupting their conversational contribution, resuming when back on the original lane.

Using a driving simulation setup, we implemented a dialogue system that realises this strategy. By employing incremental output generation, the system can interrupt and flexibly resume its output. We tested the system using a variation of a standard driving task, and found that it improved both driving performance and recall, as compared to a non-adaptive baseline system.

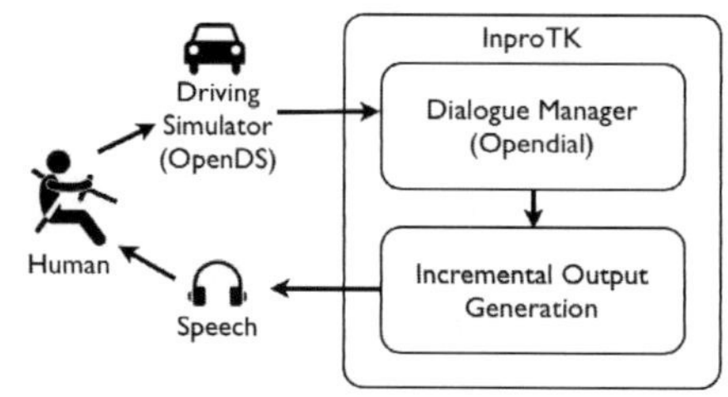

Figure 1: Overview of our system setup: human controls actions of a virtual car; events are sent to DM, which controls the speech output.

2 The Setup

2.1 The Situated In-Car System

Figure 1 shows an overview of our system setup, with its main components: a) the driving simulator that presents via computer graphics the driving task to the user; b) the dialogue system, that presents, via voice output, information to the user (here, calendar entries).

Driving Simulation For the driving simulator, we used the OpenDS Toolkit,[1] connected to a steering wheel and a board with an acceleration and brake pedal, using standard video game hardware. We developed our own simple driving scenarios (derived from the "ReactionTest" task, which is distributed together with OpenDS) that specified the driving task and timing of the concurrent speech, as described below. We modified OpenDS to pass real-time data (e.g. car position/velocity/events in the simulation, such as a gate becoming visible or a lane change) using the *mint*.tools architecture (Kousidis et al., 2013). In addition, we have bridged INPROTK (Baumann and Schlangen, 2012) with *mint*.tools via the Robotics Service Bus (RSB, Wienke and Wrede (2011)) framework.

[1]http://www.opends.eu/

Figure 2: Driver's view during experiment. The green signal on the signal-bridge indicates the target lane.

Dialogue System Using INPROTK, we implemented a simple dialogue system. The notion of "dialogue" is used with some liberty here: the user did not interact directly with the system but rather indirectly (and non-intentionally) via driving actions. Nevertheless, we used the same modularisation as in more typical dialogue systems by using a dialoge management (DM) component that controls the system actions based on the user actions. We integrated OpenDial (Lison, 2012) as the DM into INPROTK,[2] though we only used it to make simple, deterministic decisions (there was no learned dialogue policy) based on the state of the simulator (see below). We used the incremental output generation capabilities of INPROTK, as described in (Buschmeier et al., 2012).

3 Experiment

We evaluated the adaptation strategy in a driving simulation setup, where subjects performed a 30 minute, simulated drive along a straight, five-lane road, during which they were occasionally faced with two types of additional tasks: a lane-change task and a memory task, which aim to measure the driving performance and the driver's ability to pay attention to speech while driving, respectively. The two tasks occured in isolation or simultaneoulsy.

The Lane-Change Task The driving task we used is a variant of the well-known lane-change task (LCT), which is standardised in (ISO, 2010): It requires the driver to react to a green light positioned on a signal gate above the road (see Figure 2). The driver (otherwise instructed to remain in the middle lane) must move to the lane indicated by the green light, remain there until a tone is sounded, and then return again to the middle lane. OpenDS gives a *success* or *fail* result to this task depending on whether the target lane was reached within 10 seconds (if at all) and the car was in the middle lane when the signal became visible. We also added a speed constraint: the car maintained 40 km/h when the pedal was not pressed, with a top speed of 70 km/h when fully pressed. During a Lane-change, the driver was to maintain a speed of 60 km/h, thus adding to the cognitive load.

Table 1: Experiment conditions.

Lane Change	Presentation mode	Abbreviation
Yes	CONTROL	CONTROL_LANE
Yes	ADAPTIVE	ADAPTIVE_LANE
Yes	NO_TALK	NO_TALK_LANE
No	CONTROL	CONTROL_EMPTY

The Memory Task We tested the attention of the drivers to the generated speech using a simple true-false memory task. The DM generated utterances such as *"am Samstag den siebzehnten Mai 12 Uhr 15 bis 14 Uhr 15 hast du 'gemeinsam Essen im Westend mit Martin'"* (on Saturday the 17th of May from 12:15–14:15 you are meeting Martin for Lunch). Each utterance had 5 information tokens: day, time, activity, location and partner, spoken by a female voice. After utterance completion, and while no driving distraction occurred, a confirmation question was asked by a male voice, e.g. *"Richtig oder Falsch? – Freitag"* (Right or wrong? – Friday). The subject was then required to answer true or false by pressing one of two respective buttons on the steering wheel. The token of the confirmation question was chosen randomly, although tokens near the beginning of the utterance (day and time) were given a higher probability of occurrence. The starting time of the utterance relative to the gate was varied randomly between 3 and 6 seconds before visibility. Figure 3 gives a schematic overview of the task and describes the strategy we implemented for interrupting and resuming speech, triggered by the driving situation.

3.1 Conditions

Table 1 shows the 4 experiment conditions, denoting if a lane change was signalled, and what presentation strategy was used. Each condition appeared exactly 11 times in the scenario, for a total of 44 *episodes*. The order of episodes was randomly

[2] OpenDial can be found at `http://opendial.googlecode.com/`.

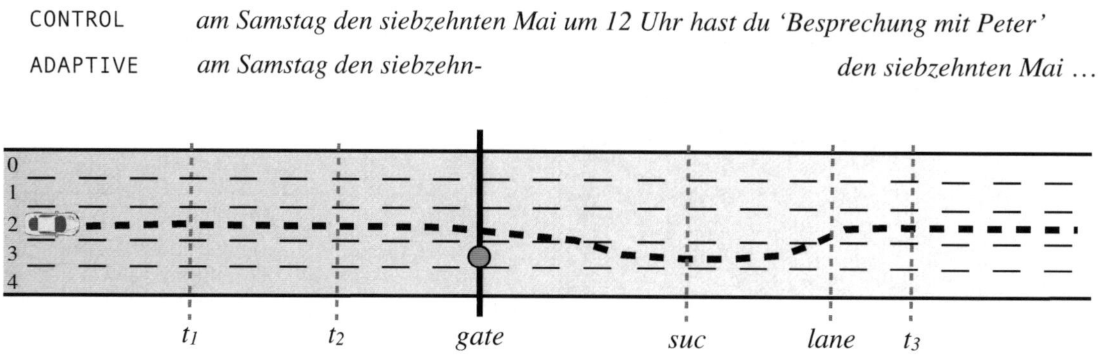

Figure 3: Top view of driving task: as the car moves to the right over time, speech begins at t_1, the gate with the lane-change indicator becomes visible at t_2, where in the adaptive version speech pauses. Successful lane change is detected at `suc`; successful change back to the middle lane is detected at `lane`, and resumes. (If no change back is detected, the interruption times out at t_3). All red-dotted lines denote events sent from OpenDS to the Dialogue Manager.

generated for each subject. With this design, subjects perceive conditions to be entirely random.

3.2 Dependent Variables

The dependent variables for the Memory task are (a) whether the subject's answer was *correct* (true/false), and (b) the *response delay*, which is the time from the end of the clarification question to the time the true or false button was pressed. For the driving task, the dependent variables are the OpenDS performance measurements *success/failure* (as defined above) and *reaction time* (time to reach the target lane).

3.3 Procedure

After signing a consent form, subjects were led into the experiment room, where seat position and audio level were adjusted, and were given written instructions. Next, the OpenDS scenario was initiated. The scenario started with 10 successive lane-change signal gates without speech, for driving training. An experimenter provided feedback during training while the subjects familiarized themselves with the driving task. Following the training gates came a clearly-marked "START" gate, signifying the beginning of the experiment to the subjects (at this point, the experimenter left). There was a "FINISH" gate at the end of the scenario. The whole stretch of road was 23 km and took approximately 30 minutes to complete. After the driving task, the subjects were given a questionnaire, which asked them to identify the information presentation strategies and assign a preference.

Table 2: Subjects' judgement of task difficulty.

Diff.	Freq.
4 (easy)	8
3	7
2	1
1 (hard)	1

Table 3: Subjects' system preference.

Preference	Freq.
ADAPTIVE	3
CONTROL	9
Neither	5

4 Results

In total, 17 subjects (8 male, 9 female, aged 19-36) participated in the study. All of the subjects were native German speakers affiliated with ANONYMIZED University. As reported in the post-test questionnaire, all held a driving license, two had previous experience with driving simulators and only one had previous experience with spoken dialogue systems. Table 2 shows the subjects' assessment of difficulty, while Table 3 shows their preference between the different strategies. Most subjects found the task relatively easy and either prefer the speech *not* to adapt or have no preference.

Memory task The overall percentages of correct answers to the system's recall questions (across all subjects) are shown in Table 4. We see that the subjects' performance in this task is considerably better when the system adapts to the driving situation (ADAPTIVE_LANE condition) rather than speaking through the lane change (CONTROL_LANE condition). In fact, the performance in the ADAPTIVE_LANE condition is closer to the control upper

Table 4: Performance in memory task per condition.

Condition	Percentage
CONTROL_EMPTY	169/180 (93.9%)
ADAPTIVE_LANE	156/172 (90.7%)
CONTROL_LANE	150/178 (84.3%)

Table 5: Success in driving task per condition (as reported by OpenDS).

Condition	Success
NOTALK_LANE	175/185 *(94.6%)*
ADAPTIVE_LANE	165/174 *(94.8%)*
CONTROL_LANE	165/180 *(91.7%)*

bound (CONTROL_EMPTY condition). We tested significance of the results using a generalized linear mixed model with CONDITION and SUBJECT as factors, which yields a p-value of 0.027 when compared against a null model in which only SUBJECT is a factor. No significant effects of between-subjects factors *gender*, *difficulty* or *preference* were found. In addition, the within-subject variable *time* did not have any significant effect (subjects do not improve in the memory task with time).

The average response delay (from the end of the recall question to the button press) per condition across all subjects is shown in Figure 4. Subjects reply slower to the recall questions in the CONTROL_LANE condition, while their performance in the ADAPTIVE_LANE condition is indistinguishable from the CONTROL_EMPTY condition (in which there is no distraction). Additionally, there is a general decreasing trend of response delay with time, which means that users get acquainted with the task (type of information, format of question) over time. Both factors (condition and time) are significant (repeated measures ANOVA, 2x2 factorial design, $F_{condition} = 3.858, p = 0.0359, F_{time} = 4.672, p = 0.00662$). No significant effects were found for any of the between-subject factors (gender, difficulty, preference).

Driving task The success rate in the lane-change task per condition is shown in Table 5. Here too we find that the performance is lower in the CONTROL_LANE condition, while ADAPTIVE_LANE does not seem to affect driving performance, when compared to the NOTALK_LANE condition. The effect is significant ($p = 0.01231$) using the same GLMM approach and factors as above.

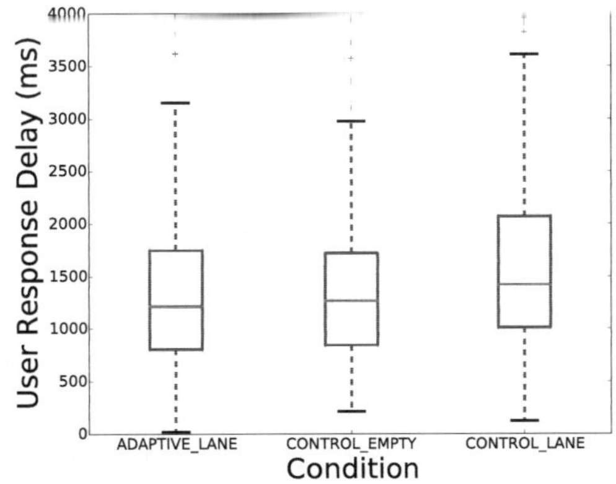

Figure 4: User answer response delay under three conditions.

5 Discussion, Conclusions, Future Work

We have developed and tested a driving simulation scenario where information is presented by a spoken dialogue system. Our system has the unique ability (compared to today's commercial systems) to adapt its speech to the driving situation: it interrupts itself when a dangerous situation occurs and later resumes with an appropriate continuation. Using this strategy, information presentation had no impact on driving, and dangerous situations no impact on information recall. In contrast, a system that blindly spoke while the driver was distracted by the lane-change task resulted in worse performance in both tasks: subjects made more errors in the memory task and also failed more of the lane-change tasks, which could prove dangerous in a real situation.

Interestingly, very few of the subjects preferred the adaptive version of the system in the post-task questionnaire. Among the reasons that they gave for this was their inability to control the interruptions/resumptions of the system. We plan to address the issue of control by allowing future versions of our system to accept user signals, such as speech or head gestures; it will be interesting to see whether this will impact driving performance or not. Further, more sophisticated presentation strategies (e.g., controlling the complexity of the generated language in accordance to the driving situation) can be tested in this framework.

Acknowledgments This research was partly supported by the Deutsche Forschungsgemeinschaft (DFG) in the CRC 673 "Alignment in Communication" and the Center of Excellence in "Cognitive Interaction Technology" (CITEC). The authors would like to thank Oliver Eckmeier and Michael Bartholdt for helping implement the system setup, as well as Gerdis Anderson and Fabian Wohlgemuth for assisting as experimenters.

References

Timo Baumann and David Schlangen. 2012. The InproTK 2012 release. In *NAACL-HLT Workshop on Future directions and needs in the Spoken Dialog Community: Tools and Data (SDCTD 2012)*, pages 29–32, Montréal, Canada.

Hendrik Buschmeier, Timo Baumann, Benjamin Dosch, Stefan Kopp, and David Schlangen. 2012. Combining incremental language generation and incremental speech synthesis for adaptive information presentation. In *Proceedings of the 13th Annual Meeting of the Special Interest Group on Discourse and Dialogue*, pages 295–303, Seoul, South Korea.

Frank A. Drews, Monisha Pasupathi, and David L. Strayer. 2004. Passenger and cell-phone conversations in simulated driving. In *Proceedings of the 48th Annual Meeting of the Human Factors and Ergonomics Society*, pages 2210–2212, New Orleans, USA.

William J. Horrey and Christopher D. Wickens. 2006. Examining the impact of cell phone conversations on driving using meta-analytic techniques. *Human Factors*, 48:196–205.

ISO. 2010. Road vehicles – Ergonomic aspects of transport information and control systems – Simulated lane change test to assess in-vehicle secondary task demand. ISO 26022:2010, Geneva, Switzerland.

Spyros Kousidis, Thies Pfeiffer, and David Schlangen. 2013. MINT.tools: Tools and adaptors supporting acquisition, annotation and analysis of multimodal corpora. In *Interspeech 2013, Lyon, France*. ISCA.

Pierre Lison. 2012. Probabilistic dialogue models with prior domain knowledge. In *Proceedings of the 13th Annual Meeting of the Special Interest Group on Discourse and Dialogue*, pages 179–188, Seoul, South Korea.

David L Strayer, Frank A Drews, and Dennis J Crouch. 2006. A comparison of the cell phone driver and the drunk driver. *Human Factors*, 48:381–91.

David L Strayer, Joel M Cooper, Jonna Turrill, James Coleman, and Nate Medeiros. 2013. Measuring cognitive distraction in the automobile. Technical report, AAA Foundation for Traffice Safety.

J Wienke and S Wrede. 2011. A middleware for collaborative research in experimental robotics. In *System Integration (SII), 2011 IEEE/SICE International Symposium on*, pages 1183–1190.

Human pause and resume behaviours for unobtrusive humanlike in-car spoken dialogue systems

Jens Edlund
KTH Speech, Music and Hearing
Stockholm
Sweden
edlund@speech.kth.se

Fredrik Edelstam
KTH Speech, Music and Hearing
Stockholm
Sweden
freede41@kth.se

Joakim Gustafson
KTH Speech, Music and Hearing
Stockholm
Sweden
jocke@speech.kth.se

Abstract

This paper presents a first, largely qualitative analysis of a set of human-human dialogues recorded specifically to provide insights in how humans handle pauses and resumptions in situations where the speakers cannot see each other, but have to rely on the acoustic signal alone. The work presented is part of a larger effort to find unobtrusive human dialogue behaviours that can be mimicked and implemented in-car spoken dialogue systems within in the EU project Get Home Safe, a collaboration between KTH, DFKI, Nuance, IBM and Daimler aiming to find ways of driver interaction that minimizes safety issues,. The analysis reveals several human temporal, semantic/pragmatic, and structural behaviours that are good candidates for inclusion in spoken dialogue systems.

1 Introduction

In-car spoken dialogue systems face specific challenges that are of little or no relevance for systems designed for other environments. The two most striking of these are (1) the very strong focus on safety in the driving situation and (2) the fact that the person who speaks to the system – its user, in other words the driver in the majority of cases – does so in an environment that may change quite drastically from the beginning of an interaction to its completion. The most straightforward source for this change is the fact that the car (and the user) moves through the environment while the dialogue progresses. The dynamic and mobile nature of the surrounding traffic adds to the complexity. Generally speaking, safety is the key concern when designing spoken dialogue systems for in-car use. While poor performance in spoken dialogue systems can clearly be a nuisance to a driver, the promise of using properly designed spoken dialogue instead of other interfaces is increased safety. This promise is based in the nature of speech: it does not require the driver to divert the use hands and eyes from the driving, and it is a mode of communication that most are quite used to and comfortable with, so should not induce great amounts of cognitive load.

We present a corpus consisting of a set of human-human dialogues recorded specifically to provide insights in how humans handle interruptions - how they pause and resume speaking - in situations where the speakers cannot see each other, but have to rely on the acoustic signal alone, and a preliminary analysis of these which reveals several candidates for inclusion in in-car spoken dialogue systems. Finally, we discuss how these can be implemented and how a selection of them are included in the Get Home Safe experiment implementation.

2 Background and related work

In a government-commissioned survey from 2011, the Swedish National Road and Transport Research Institute reviews several hundred research publications on traffic safety and the use of mobile phones and other communication devices [Kircher et al., 2011]. Amongst the most striking findings: although there is a broad consensus that visual-manual interactions (e.g. using social media or texting) with communication devices impair driving performance, bans have not had any measurable effects in terms of lowered accident rates or insurance claims. Ban compliance statistics show that bans have an effect on driver behaviour the first year, after which drivers return to their former habits. With bans being virtually ineffective, solutions must be sought elsewhere. Allowing drivers to manage more tasks using speech, which does not occupy hands and eyes, would decrease the time spent in visual-manual interaction while driving, provided that the drivers can be persuaded to use the systems.

Clearly, the systems must work well - a large proportion of errors may well put the driver at risk (e.g. Kun et al., 2007). It is also unlikely that drivers can be persuaded to use systems that do not work well. But using hand-free and eyes-free controls may not suffice. Kircher et al. (2011) notes that there is virtually no evidence that hands-free telephony is less risky than hand-held use, suggesting that the conversations in themselves may be a risk factor. Speaking to a person who is present in the car and who shares the driver's situation, however, is much safer (Peissner et al., 2011), suggesting that a system that is perceived as and behaves like a co-present human is a sensible aim. In the EU project Get Home Safe, of which this research is a part, we call such systems *humanlike proactive systems*. Where a traditional spoken dialogue system bases its decisions largely on (1) whether it has something to say, (2) what the user has just said, and (3) whether the user is speaking or is silent, a humanlike proactive system will also consider (4) the (traffic) situation, (5) the user's (driver's) estimated attention, and (6) the urgency of the task at hand, much like a passenger might.

This paper focusses on two broad types of proactive humanlike behaviours: *user controlled pacing*, referring to the ability to pause at the whim of the user in the middle of a conversation, or even an utterance, and then resume the conversation; and *situation sensitive speech*, the ability to allow the situation to affect the manner in which the system speaks. We are searching for behaviours that people use when interrupted, either by their interlocutor or by some event in their environment, and when they resume the original dialogue again. We are specifically interested in behaviours that can be implemented in the Get Home Safe architecture without major changes to existing applications. The architecture allows a central manager to instruct applications to stop where they are and maintain their inner state until instructed to either exit or continue where they were.

The task has been approached by others, albeit in different manners. Villing (2010) presents an analysis of interruptions and resumptions in human-human in-vehicle dialogues, as well as implications for future in-car dialogue systems, and Yang et al. (2011) used human-human multi-tasking dialogues that involved a poker game as the main task, and a picture game as an interrupting real-time task.

3 Method

Our goal is to collect and analyse data that will provide an insight to how a human speaker deals with interruptions in in-car dialogue (our target setting) and to find relevant behaviours that can be successfully mimicked in an in-car human-computer environment. The question can be subdivided: How does a human speaker stop speaking when faced with an (possible) interruption? How does a human speaker resume speaking after such an event? Which of these behaviours are plausible candidates for inclusion in a spoken dialogue system?

3.1 Data Collection

Setting. Collecting data from a real driving situation is time consuming, not to say dangerous when adding a secondary task. We have instead opted to simulate the key elements of interest in our dialogue recording studio – a safe recording environment consisting of several physically distinct locations that are interconnected with low and constant latency audio and video. The interlocutors were placed in different rooms, and communicated through pairs of wireless close-range microphones and loudspeakers.

Subjects. The purpose of this data collection is not for example training a recognizer, but the generation of a consistent set of candidate behaviours for implementation in a spoken dialogue system – one that contains behaviours that could all plausibly be used by the same speaker. To achieve this, we consistently use the same single male speaker in the role as the system ("speaker", hereafter) for all recordings. For the user role ("listener", hereafter), a balanced variety of speakers were used: two sets of 8 listeners, both balanced for gender, were used. None of the listeners had any previous knowledge of this research. All listeners were rewarded with one cinema ticket. They were told that those who performed the task best would earn a second ticket, and the top performers from each setup received a second ticket after the recordings were completed.

Task. The data collection was designed as a dual task experiment. The main task for the speaker was to read three short informative texts about each of three cities (Paris, Stockholm, and Tokyo), arranged so that the first is quite general, the second more specific, and the third deals with a quite narrow detail with some connection to the city. This task is equivalent to what one might expect from a tourist information system. For the listener, the main task is to listen to the city information. The listener is motivated by the knowledge that the reading of each segment - that is each of the nine informative texts - is followed by three questions on the content of the text. Their performance in answering these questions and in completing the secondary task counted towards the extra movie ticket. The secondary task was designed as follows. At irregular, random intervals, a clearly visible coloured circle would appear, either in front of the speaker or the listener. When this happened, the speaker was under obligation to stop the narration and instead read a sequence of eight digits from a list. The listener must then to repeat the digit sequence back to the speaker, after which the speaker could resume the narration.

Conditions. We considered two characteristics of in-car interruptions that we assumed would have an effect on how humans react to the interruption and to how they resume speaking after it: the source of an interruption can be either internal or external in an in-car dialogue (our target setting); and the duration and content of an interruption varies, they can be brief or even the result of a mistake, or they can be long and contentful. The condition mapping to the first of these characteristics was designed such that the coloured circle signalling an interruption was presented randomly to either the speaker, mapping to en external event visible to the system but not the driver, or to the listener, mapping to an interruption from the driver to the system (the listener had to speak up to inform the speaker that the circle was present). The second condition was designed such that in one set of eight dialogues, the coloured circle would start out yellow, and as soon as the speaker became silent, it would randomly either disappear (causing only a short interruption with light or no content, corresponding to e.g. a false alarm) or turn red, in which case the sequence of digits would be read and repeated (a contentful interruption). In the other set of eight recordings, the circle always went straight to red, and always caused digits to be read and repeated.

3.2 Analysis

Each channel of each recording was segmented into silence delimited speech segments automatically, and these were transcribed using Nuance Dragon Dictate. The transcriptions were then corrected by a human annotator, and labelled for interruptions and resumptions. In this initial analysis, we looked at temporal statistics (e.g. the durations between interruption from the listener and silence from the speaker), semantics/pragmatics (e.g. lexical choices, insertions, repetitions) and syntax (e.g. where in an utterance resumption begins).

4 Results

A categorical difference was found in the distribution of speaker response times (from the onset of a listener interruption to the offset of speaker speech) depending on whether the interruption occurred in the middle of a phrase or close to the end of the phrase. In the first case, the vast majority of the response times are distributed between 300 and 700 ms, with a clear mode around 400 ms. Only a fraction of response times are slower than 700 ms, and none except one is faster than 300 ms. Phrase final interruptions show an almost flat response time distribution, with only a very weak mode around 500 ms, and a large proportion with response times longer than 700 ms.

For lexical/pragmatic choices, we find a categorical variation for the insertion of vocalizations we somewhat lazily term filled pauses (e.g. "eh", "em") and what we equally lazily term lexical cue phrases (e.g. "right", "ok") before resumption. The existence of such insertions, as well as the choice of vocalization, is straightforwardly dependant on the contentfulness of the interruption. For short interruptions of light content, filled pauses are nearly never inserted before resumption. Lexical cue phrases are inserted, but rarely. In the typical case, the speaker goes straight back to the informational text. For long, contentful interruptions, resumption is initiated by an insertion in an overwhelming majority of cases. If the insertion consists of one vocalization only, this is nearly always a filled pause. If more than one vocalization is present, then lexical cue phrases occur frequently, but overall, lexical cue phrases are no more common here than in the case of the short interruptions.

In the case of structural comparisons, the one clear distinction we found has to do with what, if any, material is repeated at resumption, a characteristic that varies strongly with the type of interruption. For long interruptions, in every instance but a handful, the speaker either repeats the entire utterance in which the interruption occurs, or - in the few cases where an interruption occurred just as an utterance came to an end - with the next utterance. For short interruptions, resumptions also start most regularly from either the start of the current utterance or from the start of the next one. However, starts from the beginning or end of the current phrase, word, or even part of word are also frequent.

5 Discussion

We think that the three main findings presented in the results are all good candidates for implementation. The different distributions of response times suggest that if an interruption occurs centrally, in the midst of a production, the speaker stops as fast as possible - the distribution is largely consistent with reaction time distributions. Towards the end of phrases, the distribution is flat and quite different to what one would expect if reaction time was the main governing factor. The larger proportion of long response times suggests that when the speaker is close to the end of a phrase, finishing the phrase first might be preferable to stopping as soon as reaction permits. From an implementation perspective, this is quite encouraging. In order to create a behaviour consistent with this, we need to halt system speech with a reaction time of around 3-500ms. If possible (i.e. if the system knows how much time remains of its production), we may instead complete the utterance if less than, say, 700ms remains.

Seemingly, short light content interruptions need no specific signalling of resumption. If such signalling is made, it is in the form of a lexical cue phrase, such as "ok" or "right". Resumptions following longer, contentful interruptions are routinely initiated by a filled pause. This may be solely due to the speaker's need to find the correct place in the script to start over, but it is noteworthy that instead of doing this in silence, the speaker opts to vocalize. For implementation, resumptions following contentful subdialogues should start with a filled pause and perhaps a lexical cue phrase.

The straightforward interpretation of the third finding is that in the case of short interruptions, both speaker and listener have the point of interruption in fresh memory, and need no reminder, while long interruptions require the speaker to help the listener out by recapitulating what was last said. In the latter case, the system can simply start over with its last utterance (provided that it produces its synthesis on a granularity of at least utterance level).

Acknowledgments

This work was funded by the GetHomeSafe (EU 7th Framework STREP project 288667).

References

Kircher, K., Patten, C., & Ahlström, C. (2011). *Mobile telephones and other communication devices and their impact on traffic safety: a review of the literature*. Technical Report VTI 729A, Stockholm.
Kun, A., Paek, T., & Medenica, Z. (2007). The effect of speech interface accuracy on driving performance. In *Proc. of Interspeech 2007*. Antwerp, Belgium.
Peissner, M., Doebler, V., & Metze, F. (2011). *Can voice interaction help reducing the level of distraction and prevent accidents? Meta-Study on Driver Distraction and Voice Interaction*. Technical Report, Fraunhofer, Germany and CMU, USA, Aachen, Germany.
Villing, J. (2010). Now, where was I? Resumption strategies for an in-vehicle dialogue system. In *The 48th Annual Meeting of the Association for Computational Linguistics* (pp. 798-805). Sweden.
Yang, F., Heeman, P. A., & Kun, A. L. (2011). An investigation of interruptions and resumptions in multi-tasking dialogues. *Computational inguistics, 27*(1), 75-104.

Author Index